# THE CAMBRIDGE BIBLE COMMENTARY

## NEW ENGLISH BIBLE

GENERAL EDITORS

P. R. ACKROYD, A. R. C. LEANEY
J. W. PACKER

# HAGGAI, ZECHARIAH AND MALACHI

# THE BOOKS OF
# HAGGAI
# ZECHARIAH AND
# MALACHI

COMMENTARY BY

## REX MASON

*Lecturer in Hebrew and Old Testament Studies*
*Regent's Park College, Oxford*

## CAMBRIDGE UNIVERSITY PRESS

CAMBRIDGE

LONDON · NEW YORK · MELBOURNE

Published by the Syndics of the Cambridge University Press
The Pitt Building, Trumpington Street, Cambridge CB2 1RP
Bentley House, 200 Euston Road, London NW1 2DB
32 East 57th Street, New York, NY 10022, USA
296 Beaconsfield Parade, Middle Park, Melbourne 3206, Australia

© Cambridge University Press 1977

First published 1977

Printed in Great Britain at the
University Press, Cambridge

**Library of Congress cataloguing in publication data**

Bible. O.T. Haggai. English. New English. 1977.
  The Books of Haggai, Zechariah, and Malachi.

  (The Cambridge Bible commentary, New English Bible)
  Bibliography: p.
  Includes index.
  1. Bible O.T. Haggai – Commentaries. 2. Bible. O.T. Zechariah –
Commentaries. 3. Bible. O.T. Malachi – Commentaries. I. Mason, Rex,
1962. II. Bible. O.T. Zechariah. English. New English. 1977. III. Bible.
O.T. Malachi. English. New English. 1977. IV. Title. V. Series.
BS1560.M28     224'.9     77–70950

ISBN 0 521 08655 8 hard covers
ISBN 0 521 09763 0 paperback

# GENERAL EDITORS' PREFACE

The aim of this series is to provide the text of the New English Bible closely linked to a commentary in which the results of modern scholarship are made available to the general reader. Teachers and young people have been especially kept in mind. The commentators have been asked to assume no specialized theological knowledge, and no knowledge of Greek and Hebrew. Bare references to other literature and multiple references to other parts of the Bible have been avoided. Actual quotations have been given as often as possible.

The completion of the New Testament part of the series in 1967 provided the basis upon which the production of the much larger Old Testament and Apocrypha series could be undertaken. With the publication of this volume and its companion (*2 Samuel*) and the last two (*Genesis; 1 and 2 Esdras*) in the near future, the whole series is complete. The welcome accorded to the series in its earlier stages was an encouragement to the editors to follow the same general pattern throughout, and an attempt has been made to take account of criticisms which have been offered. The Old Testament volumes have included the full footnotes provided by the translators, since these are essential for the understanding of the text.

Within the severe limits imposed by the size and scope of the series, each commentator has attempted to set out the main findings of recent biblical scholarship and to describe the historical background to the text. The main

v

theological issues have also been critically discussed.

Much attention has been given to the form of the volumes. The aim is to produce books each of which will be read consecutively from first to last page. The introductory material leads naturally into the text, which itself leads into the alternating sections of the commentary.

The series is accompanied by three volumes of a more general character. *Understanding the Old Testament* sets out to provide the larger historical and archaeological background, to say something about the life and thought of the people of the Old Testament, and to answer the question 'Why should we study the Old Testament?' *The Making of the Old Testament* is concerned with the formation of the books of the Old Testament and Apocrypha in the context of the ancient Near Eastern world, and with the ways in which these books have come down to us in the life of the Jewish and Christian communities. *Old Testament Illustrations* contains maps, diagrams and photographs with an explanatory text. These three volumes are designed to provide material helpful to the understanding of the individual books and their commentaries, but they are also prepared so as to be of use quite independently.

With the completion of this project, there are many whom the General Editors wish to thank. The contributors who have produced their manuscripts and co-operated willingly in revisions suggested to them must clearly be mentioned first. With them we thank the succession of members of the staff of the Cambridge University Press, but above all Mr Michael H. Black, now Publisher at the Press, who has joined so fully in the planning and development of the series and who has been present at all the editorial meetings from the initiation of the project to its conclusion.

P.R.A.

A.R.C.L.

J.W.P.

# CONTENTS

# THE FOOTNOTES TO THE
# N.E.B. TEXT

The footnotes to the N.E.B. text are designed to help the reader either to understand particular points of detail – the meaning of a name, the presence of a play upon words – or to give information about the actual text. Where the Hebrew text appears to be erroneous, or there is doubt about its precise meaning, it may be necessary to turn to manuscripts which offer a different wording, or to ancient translations of the text which may suggest a better reading, or to offer a new explanation based upon conjecture. In such cases, the footnotes supply very briefly an indication of the evidence, and whether the solution proposed is one that is regarded as possible or as probable. Various abbreviations are used in the footnotes:

(1) Some abbreviations are simply of terms used in explaining a point: *ch(s).*, chapter(s); *cp.*, compare; *lit.*, literally; *mng.*, meaning; *MS(S).*, manuscript(s), i.e. Hebrew manuscript(s), unless otherwise stated; *om.*, omit(s); *or*, indicating an alternative interpretation; *poss.*, possible; *prob.*, probable; *rdg.*, reading; *Vs(s).*, version(s).

(2) Other abbreviations indicate sources of information from which better interpretations or readings may be obtained.

*Aq.*   Aquila, a Greek translator of the Old Testament (perhaps about A.D. 130) characterized by great literalness.

*Aram.*   Aramaic – may refer to the text in this language (used in parts of Ezra and Daniel), or to the meaning of an Aramaic word. Aramaic belongs to the same language family as Hebrew, and is known from about 1000 B.C. over a wide area of the Middle East, including Palestine.

*Heb.*   Hebrew – may refer to the Hebrew text or may indicate the literal meaning of the Hebrew word.

*Josephus*   Flavius Josephus (A.D. 37/8–about 100), author of the *Jewish Antiquities*, a survey of the whole history of his people, directed partly at least to a non-Jewish audience, and of various other works, notably one on the *Jewish War* (that of A.D. 66–73) and a defence of Judaism (*Against Apion*).

*Luc. Sept.*   Lucian's recension of the Septuagint, an important edition made in Antioch in Syria about the end of the third century A.D.

*Pesh.*   Peshitta or Peshitto, the Syriac version of the Old Testament. Syriac is the name given chiefly to a form of Eastern Aramaic used by the Christian community. The translation varies in quality, and is at many points influenced by the Septuagint or the Targums.

*Sam.*   Samaritan Pentateuch – the form of the first five books of the Old Testament as used by the Samaritan community. It is written in Hebrew in a special form of the Old Hebrew script, and preserves an important form of the text, somewhat influenced by Samaritan ideas.

*Scroll(s)*   Scroll(s), commonly called the Dead Sea Scrolls, found at or near Qumran from 1947 onwards. These important manuscripts shed light on the state of the Hebrew text as it was developing in the last centuries B.C. and the first century A.D.

*Sept.*   Septuagint (meaning 'seventy'; often abbreviated as the Roman numeral LXX), the name given to the main Greek version of the Old Testament. According to tradition, the Pentateuch was translated in Egypt in the third century B.C. by 70 (or 72) translators, six from each tribe, but the precise nature of its origin and development is not fully known. It was intended to provide Greek-speaking Jews with a convenient translation. Subsequently it came to be much revered by the Christian community.

*Symm.*   Symmachus, another Greek translator of the Old Testament (beginning of the third century A.D.), who tried to combine literalness with good style. Both Lucian and Jerome viewed his version with favour.

*Targ.*   Targum, a name given to various Aramaic versions of the Old Testament, produced over a long period and eventually standardized, for the use of Aramaic-speaking Jews.

*Theod.*   Theodotion, the author of a revision of the Septuagint (probably second century A.D.), very dependent on the Hebrew text.

*Vulg.*   Vulgate, the most important Latin version of the Old Testament, produced by Jerome about A.D. 400, and the text most used throughout the Middle Ages in western Christianity.

[ ... ]   In the text itself square brackets are used to indicate probably late additions to the Hebrew text.

(Fuller discussion of a number of these points may be found in *The Making of the Old Testament* in this series)

# THE BOOKS OF

# HAGGAI, ZECHARIAH AND MALACHI

✻   ✻   ✻   ✻   ✻   ✻   ✻   ✻   ✻   ✻   ✻   ✻   ✻

## EVENTS IN THE TIME OF HAGGAI AND ZECHARIAH

After the Second World War there was a large-scale return
of Jews to Palestine. Fired by a vision of rebuilding their
historic land and again having a home and identity of their
own, Jews from many parts of the world returned, prepared
for the sacrifice and rigour of pioneer life. Many others did
not return, but supported those who did with money and
help of many kinds. Such a return has not been universally
welcomed. Both those who were dispossessed by the return
of the Jews and neighbouring countries who, for one reason
or another, feared the emergence of a powerful Jewish nation,
have opposed it both by diplomatic persuasion and, sometimes, by direct military action.

While there are many differences between this and the
return of the Jews from the Babylonian exile of the sixth
century B.C. (for example, many then remained in Judah all
the time), it does mean that the modern reader may enter
imaginatively into the time of the prophets Haggai and
Zechariah. From a little before 600 B.C. the southern kingdom
of Judah had been under the control of the neo-Babylonian
Empire (so called to distinguish it from the early Babylonian
Empire of the second millennium B.C.). Two attempts to
achieve freedom by rebellion led to the successive captures of
Jerusalem in 597 and 586 B.C., after each of which considerable numbers of the leading members of society (including

I

King Jehoiachin in 597 B.C.) were carried away from Judah
into captivity in exile. The purpose of such a policy was that,
bereft of leadership, the community would be less able to
marshal the force and initiative needed for further rebellions.
After 586 B.C. the city, with its royal palace and temple, was
almost totally destroyed. Both for those left behind in the
ravaged territory of Judah and for those taken into exile it
must have been a desolate time of bleak and hopeless outlook.
Ps. 137 well catches the mood of some such exiles:

> 'How could we sing the LORD's song
>    in a foreign land?'         (Ps. 137: 4)

One would have expected faith in Yahweh (the nearest we
can get to the Hebrew name for God) to have succumbed.

In fact the exile was a particularly creative time in which
Yahwism proved its extraordinary resilience. In Judah the
prophet Jeremiah continued his ministry for some time before
being taken against his will to Egypt (Jer. 43: 1–7). The book
of Lamentations was composed on Judaean soil not long after
the fall of Jerusalem. Its unknown author had witnessed the
horrors of the siege. Yet the book lays bare the actual process
by which faith assimilated the disaster of the exile. In the following quotation Jerusalem, personified, confesses that the
disaster has been due to her own sin:

> 'The LORD was in the right;
>    it was I who rebelled against his commands.'
>         (Lam. 1: 18)

What had happened was seen to be not meaningless or arbi-
trary, and certainly did not mean that Yahweh was powerless.
On the contrary, if there was to be hope it could only be
because of his grace and faithfulness:

> 'The LORD, I say, is all that I have;
>    therefore I will wait for him patiently.'
>         (Lam. 3: 24)

In Babylon the prophet Ezekiel was active, together with others who were developing some of the later parts of the Pentateuch (the name given to the first five books of the Old Testament) and some of the Wisdom literature (including such works as the books of Proverbs and Job, although these are difficult to date with any precision). Either in Babylon or in Palestine others were interpreting the whole history of Israel and Judah in the light of the teaching of the prophets, in the history of Joshua–Kings. Again, the accounts of the words and deeds of the earlier prophets which now appear in the books bearing their names were being collected during this period. Above all, the prophet of Isaiah 40–55, who is called Second Isaiah because his real name is unknown to us, was quick to see signs of hope in political developments. From a lofty conception of the nature and purpose of God he promised a speedy end to their captivity and a return to their own land. He describes this event in glowing terms as an act of divine deliverance greater than the deliverance of their ancestors from Egypt, ushering in a new age of God's rule:

> 'Break forth together in shouts of triumph,
>    you ruins of Jerusalem;
> for the LORD has taken pity on his people
>    and has ransomed Jerusalem.'
>
> (Isa. 52: 9)

For all its power the neo-Babylonian Empire was a short-lived one. By 550 B.C. the Persian Cyrus had rebelled against the Median rulers and absorbed their territory into one large Medo-Persian Empire which, after further victories in the following years, stretched ominously across Babylon's northern border. If the Babylonians at first welcomed this as an end to the threat Media had posed for them, their hopes were soon to be disillusioned. In 539 B.C. Cyrus entered Babylon. The city and its empire passed into his control.

For the Jews this was to have momentous consequences. Persian policy towards her subject peoples was different from

3

that of Babylon. Perhaps it was based partly on the belief that contented subjects were less likely to rebel and, in the case of Judah, that a friendly state there would be a good buffer against the power of Egypt. Perhaps Cyrus acted also from religious motives, especially in encouraging the religious cults of his subject peoples. This policy is illustrated by his own inscriptions which speak of his restoring images and temple furnishings which had been removed after conquest. He refers to this practice at the end of one inscription known as the Cyrus Cylinder:

> 'The gods of Sumer and Akkad whom Nabonidus [the last Babylonian king] had...brought into Babylon, I at the bidding of Marduk, the great lord, made to dwell in peace in their habitations, delightful abodes. May all the gods whom I have placed within their sanctuaries address a daily prayer in my favour before Bel and Nabu, that my days may be long.'

(For details of the Cyrus Cylinder, see the companion volume to this series, *Old Testament Illustrations*, pp. 94–5.) Whatever his motives, it is clear that he permitted many displaced peoples to return to their homelands and authorized the re-building of their ruined temples and the re-establishment of their cults. For many Jews, these events in the year 538 B.C. must have seemed a remarkable fulfilment of the predictions of Second Isaiah.

The reality proved to be rather a sorry anti-climax. Scarcity of historical sources makes it difficult for us to know exactly what happened in the years following 538 B.C. We have an account in chs. 1–6 of the book of Ezra, but the author of the books of Chronicles, Ezra and Nehemiah, usually referred to as the Chronicler, composed his history long after the events and it is not clear what sources he had to draw on. It is possible that he had no contemporary sources other than the books of Haggai and Zechariah. The opening chapter of the book of Haggai, in particular, presents a grim picture of

4

the fortunes of the returned exiles. There was the inevitable hardship of any pioneers who try to rebuild a ravaged land and scratch a living from its impoverished soil. In addition, they experienced a succession of droughts and pests which led to a series of failed harvests. These, in turn, resulted in poverty and raging inflation. The Chronicler tells us that a start had been made on the rebuilding of the temple by the returned exiles. There appears to be some confusion in his sources as to who exactly began the task of rebuilding. Ezra 1: 8 and 5: 14–16 suggest that the first attempt was led by an earlier governor, Sheshbazzar. Ezra 3: 8 suggests that the work was begun under Zerubbabel, the governor of the time of Haggai and Zechariah, and this is supported by Hag. 1: 12–14 and Zech. 4: 9. The Chronicler says that the early attempt was thwarted by some who are described as 'the enemies of Judah and Benjamin' (Ezra 4: 1–5), whose efforts to become part of the rebuilt Jewish state were brusquely rejected. This suggestion of an earlier attempt at rebuilding may be due to the Chronicler's theological interpretation of events immediately after the return. He saw the exiles who returned from Babylon as the nucleus of the true Israel, the 'remnant' of old prophetic hopes. Perhaps it was unthinkable to him that these faithful representatives of the true people of God should have delayed until the time of Haggai and Zechariah before trying to rebuild the temple. Again, his description of 'the enemies of Judah and Benjamin' may be coloured by his bias against the old northern kingdom of Israel. This had broken away from Judah after the death of Solomon and he, like the authors of the books of Kings, regarded it as an apostate kingdom. On the other hand it is not impossible that an earlier attempt to rebuild the temple had been thwarted by a combination of poverty, disillusionment and hostility from outside, so that the work had to 'begin' all over again in 520 B.C.

This scene was suddenly and dramatically disturbed by violent political upheavals throughout the Persian Empire. Cyrus had been succeeded by his son Cambyses after his death in 529 B.C. In 522 B.C. Cambyses died by his own hand. The throne was seized by Darius I Hystaspes, and this led to an outbreak of rebellions throughout the empire with which Darius had to deal. It is hard to say just how these events were connected with what happened in Judah. The fact is that in the following years there was a great new impetus in the life of the community there, inspired by the preaching of Haggai and Zechariah. Their ministries began within two months of each other in 520 B.C., the second year of the reign of Darius. The picture revealed by these books is of a community under the joint leadership of a civil governor, Zerubbabel who, whatever the scope of his authority, was still subject to Persian rule, and Joshua, the high priest, as religious leader. Under their leadership the work of rebuilding the temple was begun almost immediately and completed by 515 B.C. It must have given a new sense of national identity and stability to the region, although lack of historical sources means we know nothing of the later fortunes of the two leaders, the two prophets or the community as a whole. These few years of intense and creative activity, however, made a distinctive contribution to the development of Judaism after the exile.

## HOW THE PROPHETIC BOOKS CAME TO US

Most of the Hebrew prophets originally uttered their oracles orally, very often in a poetic form which seemed to come naturally to them, perhaps from the form of education given in scribal schools. Some at least of Haggai's oracles seem to have been spoken, perhaps in poetic form. Zechariah, on the other hand (that is the prophet of chs. 1–8; see pp. 27–9, 76) may have been a writing prophet from the first, as the more studied, literary form of the night visions suggests. These visions are introduced and followed by oracular sayings of a more usual kind. Although they have probably been expanded and arranged by the editor, they may well contain a nucleus of Zechariah's preached material.

We are told that sometimes the prophets themselves committed their oracles to writing (e.g. Jer. 36). Perhaps other prophets had those who recorded their words as Baruch appears to have done for Jeremiah. Baruch, on at least one occasion, also passed on Jeremiah's oracles to others (Jer. 36: 4-10). Indeed, the very existence of the prophetic books testifies to the fact that there were those who responded to the prophet's teaching and who preserved and transmitted the tradition of his words and deeds. In doing so they played an active role in interpreting the tradition. Later the Jews came to have such a veneration for the written 'word' of scripture that they regarded no part of it as alterable. Earlier no such scruples appear to have been felt. In their record of the prophet's deeds and words they were more concerned with his particular interpretation of the events of his time. It was this which gave value and authority to what he said rather than some intrinsic verbal authority in each 'word' itself. The prophets' distinctive contribution was, after all, that they saw God at work in the events of their own time and interpreted these events in the light of faith. They saw God as working through them to an imminent final act of judgement and salvation. They offered a perspective of faith, a way of interpreting history, a particular theological insight, rather than a series of 'sayings' learned by rote. This was what those who came after them took from them, treasured and transmitted to their own contemporaries. So as time went on and new historical circumstances arose, or events did not seem to fulfil the prophet's predictions, they freely took his oracles, reinterpreted them and reapplied them in the light of the later situation. Sometimes they added to them, or set them in a context which gave a different slant to the original oracle. They were not being false to the prophet. As they saw it, they were working out his particular emphases and teaching in the new situation. Naturally, if such a process went on for a long time, the group could develop particular outlooks and emphases of its own which might modify the teaching of the original prophet at one point or another. Such a living stream of transmission of the words and memories of a prophet is often referred to as a 'school' of prophetic tradition or a 'circle' of tradition. It was in such circles that our prophetic books took shape until they finally 'solidified' into the written form in which we now have them. When they are viewed and studied in this light they can be seen as the excitingly living documents they are. They represent not just a 'static' word of God given once for all. They testify to the ongoing experience of that word among the people of God in whose life it proved to have a continuing relevance and vitality, always coming fresh and authoritative in new situations and changing circumstances.

In the book of Haggai oracles of the prophet are 'sandwiched' between introductory and concluding phrases and formulae and, on one occasion at least, an account of the effect the preaching had on the leaders and members of the community. This 'framework' is in the third person of reported speech and so is unlikely to be the work of Haggai himself. We must attribute it to the circle of tradition in which the deeds and words of Haggai were remembered and passed on. A close examination of this editorial material reveals some interesting features. It describes the community as 'the *rest* of the people', a term which is used in earlier prophetic material to designate the 'remnant', that is, the faithful nucleus of the people of God who would experience the blessings of future salvation. The term is used of them in 1: 12, 14 in an account of their obedience to the prophetic word, and again in 2: 2. This suggests that the editor saw this decisive act of obedience as constituting them as the true remnant. His description of them as those whose spirit 'the LORD stirred up' (1: 14) suggests that he saw the rebuilding of the temple as due to a divine act of renewal of the community. His use of this phrase, as well as the term 'the word of the LORD came through the prophet' (literally, 'by the hand of the prophet', 1: 1; cp. 1: 3; 2: 1), and the use of a particular word to describe the 'work' on the temple (1: 14), all answer closely to the use of words and phrases in the description of the building of the tabernacle under the leadership of Moses:

> 'Every Israelite man and woman who was minded to bring offerings to the LORD for all the work which he had commanded through Moses (literally 'by the hand of Moses') did so freely.' (Exod. 35: 29)
> 'Moses summoned...every craftsman to whom the LORD had given skill and who was willing (literally 'whose heart raised him'), to come forward and set to work.'
> (Exod. 36: 2)

This description of the building of the tabernacle comes from a part of the Pentateuch known as the 'Priestly writing'. It is so called because of its great interest in all matters of worship and its special view of the tabernacle. For the authors of the Priestly writing it was the place where Yahweh's presence was made known among his people, mediated to them through its cultic worship. The editor of the book of Haggai seems to have invested the temple with similar significance, as the words in 2: 4, which probably come from him, stress: 'I am with you, says the LORD of Hosts.'

It is also a feature of the editorial framework that, whereas in Haggai's oracles, he seems to have addressed the community as a whole, the editor suggests that he addressed primarily the leaders of the community, Zerubbabel and Joshua. This is similar to the practice of the authors of the books of Kings and Chronicles where the prophets' words are nearly always addressed to the king as representative of the community whose response is so important for the well-being of all.

Such characteristics of the editor's work suggest that Haggai's oracles were passed on in a tradition which shared some of the outlook of the authors of the Priestly writing and the Chronicler. The message of Haggai himself was that the ills the community was suffering in 520 B.C. were due to their failure to rebuild the temple. He urged the people to complete it and promised them that this would be the signal for the breaking in of God's salvation. The temple would become the centre of world pilgrimage (2: 6–9) and the rule of God, exercised through Zerubbabel, would bring peace and prosperity to his people and replace the kingdoms of the world. Although the temple was completed in 515 B.C. not all the prophet predicted came about and this must have led to some disappointment. Perhaps the editorial framework represents an interpretation of these hopes from the standpoint of the theological outlook of the Priestly writers and the Chronicler. It seems to share their view that the restored community was already experiencing the fulfilment of Haggai's prophetic hopes, at least in part. This was true when it was duly worshipping God; when it was experiencing his presence through the temple; when it was ruled by God through a properly constituted priestly leadership and was showing a proper spirit of willing obedience to his word. They obviously still treasured the oracles which spoke of something more decisive and radical in the future (e.g. Hag. 2: 20–3). But in a real sense they were already experiencing the rule of God. Let the community now show a similar willingness to obey the word of God as the contemporaries of Haggai had done and so show themselves fit to inherit all the promises of which he had spoken.

There are signs that Zech. 1–8 were also edited in similar circles. Traces of such editing are found mainly in the passages before and after the visions, perhaps because the visions were written down at a much earlier stage of their development. Even the visions, however, show traces of a developing tradition which will be discussed in the commentary. They show, for example, a tendency to emphasize the role of the priesthood, a development already apparent in the book of Haggai.

Zech. 9–14 is later than chs. 1–8, at least in its present

form, even if it contains some earlier material (see pp. 76–82). Nevertheless much of it may come from a continuing line of the tradition which gave us Zech. 1–8. This tradition evidently became more and more disillusioned with the leadership and worship of official Judaism as time went on. This resulted in a rejection of the temple worship Haggai and Zechariah had played so prominent a part in founding, and the expression of a hope for a new work of God which became increasingly radical.

The book of Malachi, whatever the time and circumstances of its origin (see pp. 137–9), showed much in common with the temper and outlook of the circle which produced Zech. 9–14, and may well have been 'taken over' by such a circle as a congenial expression of their own deep-seated criticism of contemporary Judaism.

✳   ✳   ✳   ✳   ✳   ✳   ✳   ✳   ✳   ✳   ✳   ✳   ✳

# HAGGAI

✳  ✳  ✳  ✳  ✳  ✳  ✳  ✳  ✳  ✳  ✳  ✳  ✳

## THE PROPHET HAGGAI

We know almost nothing about the prophet Haggai. We are
not even told of his parentage although his name, related to
the Hebrew word for a sacred festival, may suggest that he
was born on one of the feast days. Hag. 2: 3 does not necessarily
imply that he was an old man who had seen the first temple
himself. We cannot be sure whether he had been exiled in
Babylon and returned new to the scene in 520 B.C., or whether
he had grown up and lived in the territory of Judah. He is
steeped in the temple traditions and draws on the old language
and ideology of its worship as expressed in some of the
psalms. He sees the rebuilding of the temple as the essential
pre-condition to Yahweh's final act of salvation, of which it
will become the focal point. We cannot, therefore, assume
from the absence of reference to Jerusalem by name that he
came from the countryside outside the city. Probably only a
few fragments of his oracles have been recorded anyway.
Further, while it is true that he makes much of the agricultural consequences of the coming salvation, he also sees
important political effects as well (e.g. 2: 20–3), while the idea
of an association between judgement and famine and between
salvation and plenty is an old one (e.g. Amos 4: 7; 9: 13–15).
The truth is that Haggai was remembered for one thing only
in tradition, his prophetic activity. He is known simply as
'Haggai the prophet'.

✳  ✳  ✳  ✳  ✳  ✳  ✳  ✳  ✳  ✳  ✳  ✳  ✳

## Zerubbabel restorer of the temple

### THE MOMENT TO BUILD THE HOUSE OF THE LORD

IN THE SECOND YEAR of King Darius, on the first day 1 of the sixth month, the word of the LORD came through the prophet Haggai to Zerubbabel son of Shealtiel, governor of Judah, and to Joshua son of Jehozadak, the high priest: These are the words of the LORD of Hosts: 2 This nation says to itself that it is not yet time for the house of the LORD to be rebuilt. Then this word came 3 through Haggai the prophet: Is it a time for you to live 4 in your own well-roofed houses, while this house lies in ruins? Now these are the words of the LORD of Hosts: 5 Consider your way of life. You have sown much but 6 reaped little; you eat but never as much as you wish, you drink but never more than you need, you are clothed but never warm, and the labourer puts his wages into a purse with a hole in it. These are the words of the LORD of 7 Hosts: Consider your way of life. Go up into the hills, 8 fetch timber, and build a house acceptable to me, where I can show my glory,*a* says the LORD. You look for much and get little. At the moment when you would bring 9 home the harvest, I blast it. Why? says the LORD of Hosts. Because my house lies in ruins, while each of you has a house that he can run to. It is your fault that the 10 heavens withhold their dew and the earth its produce. So I have proclaimed a drought against land and moun- 11 tain, against corn, new wine, and oil, and all that the

[a] show my glory: *or* be honoured.

13

ground yields, against man and cattle and all the products of man's labour.

✳ Haggai encourages the people to begin the task of rebuilding the temple. They have been offering their poverty and the hardship of their lot as pioneers as excuses for their delay in starting the work. Haggai stands the argument on its head. Times are bad, he maintains, because of their failure to rebuild the temple. Once they have completed it, judgement will turn to blessing.

I. *In the second year of King Darius:* 520 B.C. (see p. 6); *the sixth month:* August/September. *Zerubbabel son of Shealtiel, governor of Judah:* Zerubbabel is a Babylonian name which adds weight to the information given in Ezra 2: 2 (= Neh. 7: 7) that he returned from the exile there to Judah, although we do not know when. According to the Chronicler he was a grandson of King Jehoiachin and so was a descendant of the royal line of David (1 Chron. 3: 17–19). It is not clear exactly what the term *governor* indicates. Clearly he was responsible to the Persian authorities. During the exile and afterwards, Judah had been part of the province of Samaria. It is not known whether it now had its own governor answerable directly to the Persian authorities, or whether it was still to some extent under the control of the governor in Samaria. In either case it is unlikely that the rulers of the province of Samaria viewed with much pleasure signs of special Persian favour to Judah. *Joshua son of Jehozadak, the high priest:* the name is spelled 'Jeshua' in the books of Ezra and Nehemiah. The Chronicler says he was descended from Seraiah who was chief priest in Jerusalem in 586 B.C. and whose son Jehozadak was taken into exile (1 Chron. 6: 14–15). That would mean that Joshua also returned to Judah from captivity in Babylon.

This verse is the editor's introduction to the brief collection of Haggai's oracles on the general theme of rebuilding the temple which follows in verses 2–11. It is he who gives us the picture of a joint rule between Zerubbabel and Joshua as civil and religious leaders of the community in Judah. He always gives the full description of their parentage and suggests that the prophetic word was addressed primarily to them. He also uses several times the formula *the word of the LORD came through* (literally 'by the hand of') *the prophet Haggai.*

2. *These are the words of the LORD of Hosts:* a formula often used by the prophets to introduce an oracle. It is known as the 'messenger formula' since it was also used by messengers to bring the message of someone like the king (e.g. 2 Kings 18: 28–9). It underlines the fact that the prophet did not believe he was acting or speaking on his own authority. This short oracle, or fragment of an oracle, is in the form known as a 'prophetic dispute' in which the prophet seems to take his hearers to court to bring an accusation against them. The phrase *LORD of Hosts* is a title often used for God in the Old Testament. It may have originated in the earlier days of Israel's battles which they saw as a holy war in which God led the Israelite armies. Alternatively it may refer to the hosts of heavenly beings who were thought to surround God, waiting to go on his errands (sometimes referred to as the Heavenly Council), or even to the 'hosts' of stars and heavenly bodies. The prophets used it to emphasize the great power of God and Haggai intends to reassure his hearers of God's power to act on their behalf. When the N.E.B. prints *LORD* in capital letters, it represents the consonants of the divine name YHWH, probably pronounced 'Yahweh'. Jews regarded the name as too sacred to pronounce, however. When the scribes inserted vowel signs between the consonants they put those for the word 'lord' ('Adonai'), showing that this was to be read. In this commentary 'Yahweh' is used for the divine name. *This nation:* literally, 'this people'. Earlier prophets used this term rather than 'my people' to imply a reproach and rejection by God (e.g. Isa. 6: 9, 10), as Haggai probably does here.

3–4. *Then this word came through Haggai the prophet:* with this phrase the editor introduces another brief oracle in which the prophet answers the people's defence in the dispute. *well-roofed houses:* the Hebrew word may mean 'panelling' or 'ceiling', but it is hardly likely that many Jews had luxurious fittings and decorations in their houses at that time. The sense seems to be, 'You have seen to it that you have a roof over your own heads but have neglected to show concern for the house of God.'

5–6. *Consider your way of life:* their excuses dismissed, the judgement which they have been experiencing is shown to be justified. For all their toil they have only a poor standard of living and even that is being eroded by inflation.

7–11. Another word of judgement with the command to build. *fetch timber:* only wood is mentioned. Either the massive stone walls of the temple still stood, having survived the fire, or the ruins provided enough stone for the rebuilding. *where I can show my glory:* this is more likely than the alternative rendering, 'where I can be honoured'. The 'glory' of God was understood as his presence revealed to his people through worship. This is why Haggai places such emphasis on the completion of the temple. He sees no 'magical' effect in the building and its worship for its own sake, an attitude which had led the earlier prophets to attack the people's dependence on the temple (Jer. 7: 4). Haggai sees the presence of God in the midst of the community's life as the only hope for its renewal.

9. *when you would bring home the harvest:* the Hebrew does not have the word for *harvest.* It may mean, 'I will reject what you bring to the (ruined) temple.' God is looking for a more total and radical response on their part.

10–11. *So I have proclaimed a drought . . . :* the outlook of traditional covenant theology, that faithfulness to God brought blessing on the land and its produce, and disobedience the opposite, is expressed in Deut. 28. Haggai appeals to the same principle in this final oracle of judgement, calling on the people to renew the covenant relationship which the completion of the temple would make possible. ✽

## THE PEOPLE'S RESPONSE

Zerubbabel son of Shealtiel, Joshua son of Jehozadak, 12
the high priest, and the rest of the people listened to what
the LORD their God had said and what the prophet
Haggai said when the LORD their God sent him, and they
were filled with fear because of the LORD. So Haggai the 13[a]
LORD's messenger, as the LORD had commissioned him,
said to the people: I am with you, says the LORD. Then 14
the LORD stirred up the spirit of Zerubbabel son of
Shealtiel, governor of Judah, of Joshua son of Jehozadak,
the high priest, and of the rest of the people; they came
and began work on the house of the LORD of Hosts their 15
God on the twenty-fourth day of the sixth month.

\* The editor gives an account of the willing response of
leaders and people. He gives greatest prominence to the
leaders, whereas the direct oracles of Haggai address the
whole community.

12–13. *the rest of the people:* the Hebrew word translated *rest*
in the prophetic literature sometimes denotes the 'remnant',
the faithful nucleus of the people of God. The editor does not
use this term until they have proved obedient to the prophetic
word. This suggests that he saw their response as fitting them
to be the true 'remnant' and so able to inherit the blessings the
prophets had promised (e.g. Jer. 23: 3). *listened to what the
LORD their God had said. . . and they were filled with fear because
of the LORD:* phrases that traditionally emphasized the
obedience called for from the people of the covenant (e.g.
Deut. 6: 2–3). Note the insistence on the divine authority of
Haggai's mission and words. *I am with you, says the LORD:*

[a] *It is possible that some verses have been misplaced and that the original
order from this point may have been* 1: 14, 15, 13; 2: 15–19, 10–14, 1–9,
20–3.

a direct quotation of an oracle of salvation from Haggai in the middle of the editorial comment. It seems to be a parallel version of an oracle recorded in more expanded form in 2: 4. Perhaps its inclusion here caused a dislocation of order to which the N.E.B. footnote refers.

14. *Then the LORD stirred up the spirit...:* another comment of the editor stressing that the response of the people was the result of the divine power which accompanied the prophetic word. Verses 14–15 closely resemble the account of the call of Moses to build the tabernacle, especially as it is recorded in Exod. 35: 29 and 36: 2 (see pp. 8–9). Since we cannot date either the editorial material in the book of Haggai or the Priestly writing of the Pentateuch we cannot speak of one influencing the other. Perhaps the editor saw a parallel in the two events as important and decisive stages in the story of God's dealings with his people, and perhaps he shared the same view of the significance of the temple as the circles which produced the Priestly writing.

15a. *on the twenty-fourth day of the sixth month:* many commentators take this to be a misplaced dating of the oracle recorded in 2: 15–19. The alteration of the order suggested in the N.E.B. footnote supports this view. If the date referred to the beginning of the building already mentioned, 'from the twenty-fourth day...' would have been more natural.  *

### ENCOURAGING THE BUILDERS

**2** In the second year of King Darius, on the twenty-first day of the seventh month, these words came from the
2 LORD through the prophet Haggai: Say to Zerubbabel son of Shealtiel, governor of Judah, to Joshua son of Jehozadak, the high priest, and to the rest of the people:
3 Is there anyone still among you who saw this house in its former glory? How does it appear to you now? Does it

not seem to you as if it were not there? But now, 4 Zerubbabel, take heart, says the LORD; take heart, Joshua son of Jehozadak, high priest. Take heart, all you people, says the LORD. Begin the work, for I am with you, says the LORD of Hosts,[a] and my spirit is present among you. Have no fear. For these are the words of the LORD of 5,6 Hosts: One thing more:[b] I will shake heaven and earth, sea and land, I will shake all nations; the treasure of all 7 nations shall come hither, and I will fill this house with glory;[c] so says the LORD of Hosts. Mine is the silver and 8 mine the gold, says the LORD of Hosts, and the glory[c] of this latter house shall surpass the glory[c] of the former, 9 says the LORD of Hosts. In this place will I grant prosperity and peace. This is the very word of the LORD of Hosts.

\* Words of encouragement to the builders by Haggai have been brought together in this section. Anyone who re-membered the first temple must by this time have been well over seventy. As in all enterprises, the excitement of starting must soon have been tested by the hardship of continuing and meanwhile the difficulties surrounding the community which had been their excuse for inactivity had not disappeared.

1–2. *In the second year of King Darius . . . :* the editor's intro-duction to Haggai's word in verse 3, the first phase of which comes from 1:15*b*.

4–5. *take heart, says the LORD . . . :* the real answer to the doubts expressed in verse 3 comes in the oracle of verses 6–9. Verses 4–5 seem to be an expansion by the editor of an original oracle of Haggai addressed to all the people. It has been inserted here because of its general similarity of theme

[a] *So Sept.; Heb. adds* the thing I covenanted with you when you came out of Egypt.
[b] *So Sept.; Heb. adds* and that a little thing.          [c] *Or* wealth.

and tone to verses 6–9. Again he records it as though addressed primarily to the leaders. *and my spirit is present among you:* the Hebrew for this phrase is used in Exodus to describe the presence of God among his people, symbolized by the pillar of cloud (e.g. Exod. 33: 10). Its use here may be to suggest that this time will be like a second Exodus, a thought under-lined in verse 5, which is relegated in the N.E.B. to a footnote because many scholars believe it is a gloss. The 'gloss' explicitly declares that the relationship with God they know even now as they build and afterwards is a fulfilment of the promises made when the covenant was established with their fathers following the deliverance from Egypt. If, as a reference to Haggai's words in 1: 13 might suggest, the reference to *spirit* is due to editorial expansion, the editor may be reminding readers of his own time of God's power to bring Haggai's prophecies to pass in the difficulties they are facing.

6. *I will shake heaven and earth:* earthquake and storm were traditionally thought of as phenomena accompanying an appearance of God, especially in his appearance to Moses at Mount Sinai (Exod. 19: 16–18). The prophets often used similar terms to describe an appearance of God to the whole world in a final act of judgement and salvation (e.g. Isa. 24: 19–20).

7. *the treasure of all nations shall come hither:* the Hebrew word translated *treasure* means 'desire', but because the verb it governs is plural most commentators follow the Septuagint (the Greek translation of the Old Testament made before the Christian era) in altering the Hebrew vowel pointing to read the plural. 'The desirable things' then come to mean 'trea-sures', although the N.E.B. has retained a singular form of the noun. It was the Vulgate (the Latin translation of the Old Testament made in the Christian era) which first gave this a messianic interpretation which is certainly not intended in the text. There is no suggestion that this will be forced tribute. The nations will see this great act of God and bring their offerings to the rebuilt temple in Jerusalem to worship him, a thought very close to Isa. 60: 6:

'Camels in droves shall cover the land,
   dromedaries of Midian and Ephah,
 all coming from Sheba
 laden with golden spice and frankincense,
   heralds of the LORD's praise.'

There is, therefore, just a glimpse of a universalism in Haggai, that is, a belief that people of other nations will also share God's salvation. *I will fill this house with glory:* the context may imply that *glory* here means primarily 'wealth' as the N.E.B. footnote suggests. Yet behind it may be the thought that the wealth of the nations will be brought to the temple because it is the place where God reveals himself in his *glory*. The prophet insists that all this makes the hard task of rebuilding abundantly worthwhile.

9. *In this place...:* this was probably a separate oracle relating either to the temple or to Jerusalem. *prosperity and peace:* these two words translate the one Hebrew word *peace* in an attempt to render its very full content. It signifies all that is included in God's salvation of his people. ✶

A PRIESTLY DIRECTIVE

In the second year of Darius, on the twenty-fourth day 10 of the ninth month, this word came from the LORD to the prophet Haggai: These are the words of the LORD of 11 Hosts: Ask the priests to give their ruling: If a man is 12 carrying consecrated flesh in a fold of his robe, and he lets the fold touch bread or broth or wine or oil or any other kind of food, will that also become consecrated? And the priests answered, 'No.' Haggai went on, But if 13 a person defiled by contact with a corpse touches any one of these things, will that also become defiled? 'It will', answered the priests. Haggai replied, So it is with this 14 people and nation and all that they do, says the LORD; whatever offering they make here is defiled in my sight.

✳ A request addressed to the priests for a ruling on a cultic matter is made the occasion for an oracle of warning to the people by Haggai.

12-13. *will that also become consecrated?:* question and answer establish the fact that ritual 'defilement' can be caught by contact with something unclean (the law about contact with a corpse is found in Num. 19: 11-13) but ritual purity cannot be passed on by mere contact. It is true that the priest's robe was made 'holy' by contact with the 'holy' flesh of the sin offering (Lev. 6: 26-7) but such 'holiness' could not be passed on outside the sanctuary.

14. *So it is with this people...:* Haggai's application of the ruling. Three suggestions have been made to explain its meaning:

(a) The oracle dates from before the building of the temple and says that none of the offerings of the people is acceptable to God because of the lack of a properly sanctified altar. In this case the date must be in error.

(b) The phrase *this people and nation* refers not, as in 1: 2, to the returned exiles, but to the mixed population of the old northern kingdom whom the Chronicler records as having offered to help in the rebuilding of the temple (Ezra 4: 1-3). This oracle was Haggai's instruction to reject the offer.

(c) It is a warning to the community engaged in the rebuilding that the mere presence of the temple would not automatically guarantee the holiness of the community. In the manner of the earlier prophets Haggai would be saying that repentance and a right way of life alone would invest the temple and its worship with true meaning. The Septuagint seems to have understood it in this way for it adds a quotation from Amos 5: 10, 'You have hated him who reproved in your gate', a reference to the unjust who hate a 'straight' judge in their courts ('gate') who could not be bribed. ✳

## PROMISE OF FUTURE BLESSING

And now look back over recent times down to this day: 15
before one stone was laid on another in the LORD's temple, 16
what was your plight? If a man came to a heap of corn
expecting twenty measures, he found but ten; if he came
to a wine-vat to draw fifty measures,[a] he found but
twenty. I blasted you and all your harvest with black 17
blight and red and with hail, and yet you had no mind to
return to me, says the LORD. Consider, from this day 18
onwards, from this twenty-fourth day of the ninth month,
the day when the foundations of the temple of the LORD
are laid, consider: will the seed still be diminished[b] in the 19
barn? Will the vine and the fig, the pomegranate and the
olive, still bear no fruit? Not so, from this day I will bless
you.

✶ 15. *And now look back over recent times. . . :* this oracle shows
many parallels to those of ch. 1. Poor harvests are seen as God's
judgement for failure to rebuild the temple; the act of building is seen as a turning-point in their fortunes; and there is the
same vivid style of question and answer, a kind of running
dialogue with the prophet's hearers. If the date given in
1: 15*a*, 'on the twenty-fourth day of the sixth month', was
once the introduction to this oracle, it would have been
spoken at the laying of the foundation-stone, an occasion it
would fit very well. In that case the date of verse 18, 'from
this twenty-fourth day of the ninth month' must be a gloss,
perhaps inserted when the oracle was misplaced from the end
of ch. 1 to bring it into line with 2: 10–14, of which it was
thought to have been a part.

[a] *So Pesh.; Heb. adds* winepress.
[b] diminished: *prob. rdg.; Heb. om.*

23

17. *I blasted you and all your harvest:* this seems to echo Amos 4: 9. It may have been inserted by someone later than Haggai to show that what happened after the exile fulfilled the teaching of the earlier prophets. The same lack of faithfulness shown by their fathers had brought the same kind of judgement on them. Nevertheless, their obedience now would usher in the age of salvation also predicted by the prophets. If so, the commentator was very accurately representing the heart of Haggai's message.

19. *consider: will the seed still be diminished...?:* the Hebrew is obscure and can be taken in two ways: (a) the land is already bearing the signs of God's blessing, and thus the phrase is an assurance to the people by the prophet: (b) it is a statement of the people's objections, 'There is no sign of this new age yet', to which Haggai replies, 'From now on all will be different.' This perhaps suits Haggai's question-and-answer style better. *

A PROMISE CONCERNING ZERUBBABEL

20 On that day, the twenty-fourth day of the month, the
21 word of the LORD came to Haggai a second time: Tell Zerubbabel, governor of Judah, I will shake heaven and
22 earth; I will overthrow the thrones of kings, break the power of heathen realms, overturn chariots and their riders; horses and riders shall fall by the sword of their
23 comrades. On that day, says the LORD of Hosts, I will take you, Zerubbabel son of Shealtiel, my servant, and will wear you as a signet-ring; for you it is that I have chosen. This is the very word of the LORD of Hosts.

* This final oracle shows the great hopes Haggai attached to Zerubbabel.

21. *I will shake heaven and earth:* the language is similar to that of 2: 6–9. There, God's shaking of the world was as-

sociated with the completion of the temple. Here it is associated with the establishment of a descendant of David on the throne as one sign of the new age.

22. *I will...break the power of heathen realms...:* the language is militaristic, but it is characteristic of the language of the psalms which speak of God's universal kingship (e.g. Ps. 46: 8–10).

23. *my servant...signet-ring:* the king was often referred to as God's *servant* and the term *signet-ring* was used of King Jehoiachin by Jeremiah (Jer. 22: 24). The language of the oracle shows that Haggai saw Zerubbabel as a messianic figure and therefore envisaged political independence for the community in the new age. How far this was associated with the political upheavals throughout the Persian Empire early in the reign of Darius is difficult to say. It is significant that in the editorial framework Zerubbabel is seen only as a builder of the temple, in much the same way as the Chronicler saw David as more of a cultic than a military figure. No direct oracle of Haggai has been recorded (2: 4 has been expanded by the editor) which spoke of Joshua. He figures only in the editorial framework which may suggest that by the time the oracles of Haggai were edited, the priesthood had begun to come into greater prominence, a process which has gone farther in the editing of Zech. 1–8.  ✳

✳   ✳   ✳   ✳   ✳   ✳   ✳   ✳   ✳   ✳   ✳   ✳   ✳

### THE MESSAGE OF THE BOOK OF HAGGAI

Although the temple was completed by 515 B.C., events cannot have fulfilled such high expectations as Haggai predicted. We know too little of the history of the next few decades to be able to say what happened to Zerubbabel and how the community fared. To that extent a quick reading of Haggai's prophecy would lead us to say he was wrong. However, we see in the editorial framework, how one man or group interpreted his words in the light of faith. They seized on his central message that what matters to any community is its relationship to God and they presented the message of Haggai to the people of their own day with this as its main challenge. They argued that the great hopes of the earlier prophets were finding their fulfilment in the life of the community, the 'remnant', organized as a 'theocracy' under properly ordained leadership and duly worshipping God in the temple. This 'true' Israel could confidently await the final outcome of God's purpose for them and the whole world in the light of the experience of his grace that they already knew. This earliest interpretation of the words and ministry of Haggai to come down to us is a not ignoble one. It suggests that Haggai's message was not without its relevance for the community of faith of a later time. It may point to one way in which the promises of the prophets concerning the last things can be understood and appropriated in a different age. *

* * * * * * * * * * * * *

# ZECHARIAH 1-8

✳ ✳ ✳ ✳ ✳ ✳ ✳ ✳ ✳ ✳ ✳ ✳ ✳

## THE PROPHET ZECHARIAH

Almost as little is known of the prophet Zechariah as of his contemporary Haggai. His parentage is mentioned in 1: 1 but there is some confusion. In Neh. 12: 16 a Zechariah is mentioned, of the family of Iddo. In Neh. 12: 4 Iddo is said to have been a priest who came with Zerubbabel and Joshua to Jerusalem from Babylon. No mention is made there of Berechiah who is said in Zech. 1: 1 to have been Zechariah's father. This has led some to think that the name Berechiah has been brought into the verse on the basis of Isa. 8: 2 which speaks of a Zechariah, a son of Jeberechiah who was a contemporary of Isaiah. If so, such an addition must have been a mistake or some exegetical purpose was intended which is not clear to us now. What does seem to emerge is that Zechariah, like Ezekiel, was called to be a prophet but also came from a priestly family.

Nothing can be said confidently of his age, but some of the visions may possibly have been uttered originally earlier in Babylon (see commentary), which would suggest a ministry stretching back before 520 B.C. Some have thought that the oracles he uttered calling for right ethical living (e.g. 7: 8–13; 8: 16–17) were added to the visions later. This would have been done when his predictions of what was to follow the completion of the temple did not seem to have been fulfilled, and would imply a continuation of his ministry afterwards. Even if the oracles were meant to serve this purpose, however, they could have been added by someone else. We cannot make any certain deductions from them about the length of his ministry. According to the dates given in the book

Zechariah began his ministry in 520 B.C., two months after Haggai, and continued until 518 B.C.

Though strongly conscious of his own divine commission as a prophet (cp. 2: 11; 4: 9; 6: 15) he shows dependence on earlier prophecy, especially that of Ezekiel. This dependence begins to characterize prophecy after the exile as though it were felt that the authoritative word of prophecy had been given by then. That does not mean that originality and invention were running dry, but rather that the words of the earlier prophets were seen as still relevant to the later time, and were receiving a new application in contemporary events. Zechariah was steeped in the traditions of Zion and the temple which saw Jerusalem as the city which God had chosen for himself and where he dwelt in the midst of his people. He, like Haggai, sees the completion of the rebuilding of the temple as the decisive turning-point which will usher in the new age of salvation, but he sees that completion more as a divine gift than as the sign of the people's penitence. He stresses, in a way that the recorded oracles of Haggai do not, the divine grace in cleansing the land and the community, a grace which makes the response of the people possible. Like Haggai also he sees an important role for Zerubbabel, although it is not quite as clear as is sometimes claimed how far he explicitly invested Zerubbabel with a messianic role. In the same way it is difficult to know how he saw the part of Joshua the high priest. He may have cast Zerubbabel and Joshua in a dual role alongside each other. Yet we shall see signs that the tradition has been passed on among those who were anxious to elevate the role of the priesthood and to limit the role of Zerubbabel to that of temple builder, and no more. They also cast hopes of a coming messianic figure into the future and saw those hopes to depend meanwhile on the faithful, continuing role of the priesthood. The final visions of ch. 8 are more explicitly universalistic in outlook than Haggai.

### THE STRUCTURE AND CONTENTS OF
### ZECHARIAH 1–8

The outline of these chapters is clear:

1: 1–6. A warning to contemporaries to heed the words of the prophet in the light of what followed the rejection of the earlier prophets by their forefathers.

1: 7 – 6: 15. A series of eight 'night visions' proclaiming the coming age of salvation.

7: 1 – 8: 23. A number of oracles in the style of the earlier prophets calling for right ethical living, beginning with a narrative from the prophet's ministry.

There are some signs, especially in the first and final sections, that the book has been edited in a similar way, and from a similar viewpoint, to the editing of the book of Haggai. The visions themselves do not bear such obvious traces of editing perhaps because, as has been suggested already, they were written from the first, or from a very early stage of their development. The contents of the visions suggest that some of them may originally have been composed at different times but were then brought together under the one dating of 1: 7 and related to the theme of the rebuilding of the temple, probably by the prophet himself. In addition there are interspersed throughout them a number of oracles – 1: 16, 17; 2: 6–13; 3: 8–10; 4: 6–10*a*; 6: 9–15 – which may have been uttered originally independently of the visions. If so, visions and oracles may have been joined later either by the prophet or an editor.

### THE NIGHT VISIONS

We may well ask why the prophet brings his message in the form of 'visions of the night'. Many of the earlier prophets such as Amos, Isaiah of Jerusalem, Jeremiah and, above all, Ezekiel, had received some of their revelations through visions. Further, the idea of the prophet as a 'watchman' who looks out to see signs of God's activity had been used by some of them. For example, Habbakuk said

> 'I will stand at my post,
> I will take up my position on the watch-tower,
> I will watch to learn what he will say through me'

And God commands him,

> 'Write down the vision, inscribe it on tablets...
>   for there is still a vision for the appointed time...
>     If it delays, wait for it;
>     for when it comes will be no time to linger.'
>                                                   (Hab. 2: 1–3)

Ezekiel saw his role in similar terms: 'Man, I have made you a watchman for the Israelites' (3: 17). This gives a special interest to a passage in Isaiah:

> 'All day long I stand on the Lord's watch-tower
> and night after night I keep my station.
> See, there come men in a chariot, a two-horsed chariot.
>   And a voice calls back:
> Fallen, fallen is Babylon'                          (Isa. 21: 8–9)

To this has been added a fragment of another oracle on a similar theme:

> 'One calls to me from Seir:
> Watchman, what is left of the night?'     (verse 11)

There is considerable obscurity about these last two oracles and, clearly, they are later than Isaiah of Jerusalem. They have to do with the longing for the end of the sufferings of the exile and the expected fall of Babylon. The connection with chariots and horses is interesting in view of their role in the first and last visions of Zechariah. We cannot assume any literary dependence between the two. Nevertheless both draw on imagery of night as the time of suffering and distress with God's deliverance coming with the light of morning, so prominent in some of the psalms (e.g. Pss. 30: 5; 46: 5). This may suggest the idea of the prophet as a watchman at his post during the long night of distress, detecting the first signs of the light of God's intervention to deliver his people. Zechariah may have been drawing on such motifs and traditions to interpret his own role. This was to bring to his people the good news of the dawn of God's day after the long night of their suffering. It would not do on this account to dismiss the 'night visions' as a mere literary convention, if by that we mean that they do not reflect a genuine conviction of God's message. Just as great poets can use conventional forms, such as the sonnet, to express genuine feeling, so the true prophet could express what he felt intensely and deeply to be true through stereotyped forms.

There are some slight variations of structure within the visions but, for the most part, they follow a simple pattern: (a) an introduction; (b) a description of the vision; (c) the prophet asks concerning the meaning of the vision; (d) the interpreting angel gives the explanation. The one vision to diverge sharply from this pattern is the fourth, in ch. 3, and this has led a number of scholars to suggest that it has been added later to an original series of seven visions. The arguments are discussed in the commentary.

\*   \*   \*   \*   \*   \*   \*   \*   \*   \*   \*   \*   \*

# Zechariah's commission

## 'LEARN FROM THE PAST!'

IN THE EIGHTH MONTH of the second year of Darius, 1 the word of the LORD came to the prophet Zechariah son of Berechiah, son of Iddo: The LORD was very angry 2

3 with your forefathers. Say to the people, These are the
words of the LORD of Hosts: Come back to me, and I will
4 come back to you, says the LORD of Hosts. Do not be like
your forefathers. They heard the prophets of old proclaim, 'These are the words of the LORD of Hosts: Turn
back from your evil ways and your evil deeds.' But they
did not listen or pay heed to me, says the LORD. And
5 where are your forefathers now? And the prophets, do
6 they live for ever? But the warnings and the decrees with
which I charged my servants the prophets – did not these
overtake your forefathers? Did they not then repent and
say, 'The LORD of Hosts has treated us as he purposed; as
our lives and as our deeds deserved, so has he treated us'?

* Before the visions themselves comes this call to heed the
lessons of the past and to repent.

1. *In the eighth month of the second year of Darius:* October/
November 520 B.C., that is, two months later than Haggai
had begun preaching.

2. *The LORD was very angry...:* verse 2 interrupts the
sequence of the commission in verses 1 and 3. It conforms to
the practice of the editor in the book of Haggai of putting
together the word of God to the prophet and the prophet's
address to the people (e.g. Hag. 1: 1–3; 2: 1–3).

3. *Come back to me...:* the content and form of the message
are very close to 2 Chron. 30: 6–9, which suggests that this
was familiar hortatory material used in temple preaching at
the time of the Chronicler. Possibly this may indicate that the
nucleus of such a call by Zechariah to his contemporaries has
become the basis of a call to the editor's contemporaries of a
later time; and this exegetical purpose has led to the placing
of these verses as an introduction to the visions.

5. *And the prophets, do they live for ever?:* their fathers have
gone, swept away by God's judgement for their sins. But

although the prophets, the messengers of that word of judgement, have also passed from the scene, God's word remains
always true and relevant. The whole passage illustrates the
fact that later dependence on earlier prophecy sprang not
from slavish imitation but from living faith in the continuing
relevance and vitality of the word of God.

6. *did not these overtake your forefathers?*: according to the
present Hebrew text the reference is to the judgements that
came upon their fathers for their disobedience. A very
plausible emendation, however, would give instead 'have not
these overtaken you?', thus relating the whole message of the
prophet to his hearers. *Did they not then repent and say . . . ?*: the
N.E.B. takes this as a question. There is nothing in the Hebrew
text to suggest that it is a question, however. If in fact Zechariah
has been addressing his contemporaries and saying, 'Have not
these disasters overtaken you?', then this could be a statement
of the editor's, describing the repentance of Zechariah's
hearers: 'So they repented and said, The LORD of Hosts has
treated us as he purposed...' This would then correspond
exactly to the description of the response of Haggai's hearers
in the book of Haggai (1: 12–14). This explanation seems the
more likely, since, if the reference is back to the fathers, we
are left with a contradiction between verses 4*b* and 6*b* which
give conflicting accounts of the fathers' response to the words
of the prophets.

It is difficult to decide whether this section stems from
Zechariah himself or the editor. The visions are not only
introduced by such hortatory material but concluded by it as
well (6: 15*b* and ch. 7). It is certainly not inconsistent that the
prophet should both have brought the good news of God's
coming act of salvation in the visions and called on the people
to prepare for that act and prove worthy of it by their response. The oracles in chs. 7 and 8 suggest that Zechariah was
remembered in tradition for such preaching. We do not need
to suppose that he turned to such exhortation only when he
found that his predictions were not fulfilled. However, there

are indications of the editor's activity, as the commentary has shown. This may suggest that the editor has extended a number of the prophet's oracles into sermon-type material to indicate how faithful the contemporaries of Zechariah proved (as he had done in the book of Haggai) and to relate the prophet's message to his own contemporaries. Let them also prove obedient and faithful in the same way, that they may experience the promises of which the prophet had spoken to his generation. ✶

# *Eight visions with their interpretations*

## FIRST VISION – GOD WILL ACT TO RESTORE JERUSALEM

7 ON THE TWENTY-FOURTH DAY of the eleventh month, the month Shebat, in the second year of Darius, the word of the LORD came to the prophet Zechariah son of Berechiah, son of Iddo.

8 Last night I had a vision. I saw a man on a bay horse standing among the myrtles in a hollow; and behind him 9 were other horses, black, dappled,[a] and white. 'What are these, sir?' I asked, and the angel who talked with me 10 answered, 'I will show you what they are.' Then the man standing among the myrtles said, 'They are those whom the LORD has sent to range through the world.' 11 They reported to the angel of the LORD as he stood among the myrtles: 'We have ranged through the world; the

[a] black, dappled: *prob. rdg., cp. Sept.; Heb.* bay, sorrel.

whole world is still and at peace.' Thereupon the angel of 12
the LORD said, 'How long, O LORD of Hosts, wilt thou
withhold thy compassion from Jerusalem and the cities of
Judah, upon whom thou hast vented thy wrath these
seventy years?' Then the LORD spoke kind and com- 13
forting words to the angel who talked with me, and the 14
angel said to me, Proclaim, These are the words of the
LORD of Hosts: I am very jealous for Jerusalem and Zion.
I am full of anger against the nations that enjoy their 15
ease, because, while my anger was but mild, they heaped
evil on evil. Therefore these are the words of the LORD: 16
I have come back to Jerusalem with compassion, and my
house shall be rebuilt in her, says the LORD of Hosts, and
the measuring-line shall be stretched over Jerusalem.
Proclaim once more, These are the words of the LORD 17
of Hosts: My cities shall again overflow with good things;
once again the LORD will comfort Zion, once again he
will make Jerusalem the city of his choice.

* 7. *On the twenty-fourth day of the eleventh month...in the
second year of Darius:* February 519 B.C., two months after
Haggai had predicted a shattering cosmic upheaval (Hag. 2:
20–3). The verse is editorial, as the awkward transition to the
first-person account of verse 8 shows. Logically, verse 7
would make God the speaker in verse 8 whereas it is the
prophet who speaks there. It is suggested by 4: 1 that the date
is meant to govern all the visions. In fact, although they have
now been joined in a series and all related to one theme and
occasion, there are indications within them of a more varied
origin.

8. *Last night I had a vision:* for a discussion of the 'night-
vision' form of oracle, see pp. 29–31. *I saw a man on a bay horse
standing...:* there seems to be some confusion over the princi-

pal actors in the scene which follows. There is the leader of the patrolling horsemen (verse 10 need not imply that he was thought of there as standing on his own feet without a horse); there is the angel who spoke to the prophet interpreting the vision (verses 9, 13); and in verse 11 there is a reference to the 'angel of the LORD' who 'stood among the myrtles'. It may be that some confusion crept into the text when an originally independent vision was brought into the series as a whole, especially perhaps in an attempt to relate it to the final vision in 6: 1–8. But if the patrolling horsemen are seen as angelic messengers who go about the earth as members of the Council of Heaven (see p. 15), then their leader could be spoken of both as a 'man' and as 'the angel of the LORD'. Angels are so spoken of elsewhere in the Old Testament (e.g. Gen. 19: 1, 5). Then the figure of verses 8, 10, 11 and 12 could be the same and the action becomes clearer. The prophet sees this figure at the head of his patrol (verse 8). He asks the interpreting angel what the vision means, and the angel says that he will show him (verse 9). The leader of the patrol explains who the riders are (verse 10). The members of the patrol report to him (verse 11). Either he, or the interpreting angel, probably the latter, cries out in intercession to God (verse 12) and God gives him a reply which he passes on to the prophet (verses 13–15). *among the myrtles in a hollow:* the scene is meant to portray the entrance to heaven. It has been suggested that behind the imagery are mythical concepts, since in some literature of the ancient Near East, myrtles indicate the abode of the gods. However, its use in a prophetic passage such as Isa. 55: 12–13 announcing the age of salvation, may have been more influential:

'Before you mountains and hills shall break into cries of joy,
and all the trees of the wild shall clap their hands,
pine-trees shall shoot up in place of camel-thorn,
myrtles instead of briars'

*hollow* sometimes symbolizes the distress of the people of God, as in Ps. 88: 6:

> 'Thou hast plunged me into the lowest abyss,
> in dark places, in the depths (hollows).'

Possibly, therefore, behind the symbolism of the vision is the thought that God is about to intervene to deliver his people from their distress into the new age of salvation. *and behind him were other horses:* the colours are not significant, but the number four suggests that God's messengers patrol all the quarters of the earth, all of which is thus open to his gaze and under his control.

11. *the whole world is still and at peace:* in a bad sense for the people of God. In its present context it would suggest that the upheavals connected with the accession of Darius to the Persian throne had passed without sign of the earth-shattering events foretold by Haggai. If the vision had been first uttered in the time of the exile then the original reference would have been to the absence of signs of those political events which were to lead to the fall of Babylon and the release of the captives.

12. *How long, O LORD of Hosts...?:* the familiar cry of the laments used in Israel's worship (e.g. Ps. 6: 3). *these seventy years?:* Jeremiah had predicted a judgement by exile lasting seventy years (Jer. 25: 11; 29: 10). It was probably meant as a round number rather than a literal prediction. Reference to it here suggests that the origin of this vision is to be sought in the time of the exile.

15. *I am full of anger against the nations...:* this was the climax of the original vision before the oracles of verses 16–17 were added. It confirms the impression given elsewhere in the vision that it related originally, not to the rebuilding of the temple, but to the situation of the exile and the oppression of Israel by such countries as Babylon. It was first intended, like the preaching of Second Isaiah, to bring hope to the exiles.

16. *Therefore these are the words of the LORD:* this introductory formula shows that this was originally an independent

oracle. *I have come back to Jerusalem:* this corresponds to Ezekiel's vision of God returning in his glory to the city he had abandoned (Ezek. 43: 1–5). It is not clear whether Zechariah thought this already had happened, or uses what is called a 'prophetic perfect' which announces a future event that is felt to be so certain that it can be spoken of as if it were already accomplished. The account of God's return to Jerusalem in Ezek. 43: 1–5 follows the description of the measuring of Jerusalem (Ezek. 40–2) and it is probably the influence of this which accounts for the reference to the measuring of the city here. Unlike 2: 1–5 the measuring here signifies the rebuilding of the ruined city. This oracle was probably added when the vision was brought into its place in the series to relate it clearly to the time of the rebuilding of the temple. Note that for Zechariah, the rebuilding is the result of the divine initiative rather than a test of the people's obedience.

17. *My cities shall again overflow with good things:* another Zion-centred oracle which speaks of the bringing in of the treasures of the nations (cp. Hag. 2: 7) and of God's choice of Jerusalem. God's faithfulness to his promises which they had celebrated in their worship (e.g. Pss. 46, 48) is the ground of their hope at this time of new beginning. ✲

### SECOND VISION – THE OPPRESSOR NATIONS TO BE OVERTHROWN

18,*ᵃ* 19   I lifted my eyes and there I saw four horns. I asked the angel who talked with me what they were, and he answered, 'These are the horns which scattered Judah*ᵇ* and
20, 21 Jerusalem.' Then the LORD showed me four smiths. I asked what they were coming to do, and he said, 'Those horns scattered Judah and Jerusalem*ᶜ* so completely that

[*a*] 2: 1 in Heb.          [*b*] *Prob. rdg.; Heb. adds* Israel.
[*c*] and Jerusalem: *so some Sept. MSS.; Heb. om.*

no man could lift his head. But these smiths have come to reunite them and to throw down the horns of the nations which had raised them against the land of Judah and scattered its people.'

✶ A brief account of a vision which leads to the same promise as the first vision originally did in 1: 15, only making more explicit the fact that the restoration of Jerusalem and Judah will be preceded by the overthrow of the oppressor nations.

18. *I saw four horns:* horns are often mentioned in the Old Testament as symbols of power and especially of royal power (e.g. Jer. 48: 25; Mic. 4: 13). The number four probably corresponds to the four horsemen of the first vision and the four chariots of the last, and indicates the totality of heathen powers which have oppressed the people of God. The kings of the ancient Babylonian Empire sometimes referred to themselves as 'king of the four rims of the earth'.

19. *which scattered Judah and Jerusalem:* a phrase which reveals that the oppression particularly in view is the exile and suggests that this vision, like the first, originated during the exile. As the N.E.B. footnote shows, the term 'Israel' is included in the Hebrew text, but as it does not recur in verse 21, many regard it as a gloss. It may be early commentary by someone who had in mind Ezekiel's prophecy of an ultimate reunion between the former kingdoms of north and south (Ezek. 37: 15–23), or it may express the editor's view that the community of Judah and Jerusalem was the true 'Israel'. The Chronicler shared this view, sometimes using the term 'Israel' when he was clearly referring to Judah (e.g. 2 Chron. 11: 3).

20. *Then the LORD showed me four smiths:* the picture of smiths as agents of divine judgement appears in Ezekiel's prophecy. The Amorites are warned

'I will hand you over to brutal men,
    skilled in destruction.'          (Ezek. 21: 31)

the latter phrase meaning literally, 'smiths of destruction'. It may be that, as in Mic. 4: 13, the horns were thought of as being made of iron, which would make the reference to smiths more appropriate. In Isa. 54: 16-17 Babylon is pictured as a smith whom God created to judge Israel. As in that passage the idea in this vision is of a reversal of former judgement. Now it is the turn of the oppressors to be judged.

21. *But these smiths have come to reunite them. . . :* the N.E.B. translators have read another word for the Hebrew verb 'to terrify' which stands in the text. 'Jerusalem and Judah' have been taken as the object of the verb since 'them' is masculine and cannot refer to the 'horns', which are feminine in Hebrew. Since 'them' may mean 'the nations' generally, however, it is better to read '. . .and have come to terrify them'. ✳

THIRD VISION – GOD WILL ENLARGE AND PROTECT
JERUSALEM

**2** I lifted my eyes and there I saw a man carrying a
2 measuring-line. I asked him where he was going, and he said, 'To measure Jerusalem and see what should be its
3 breadth and length.' Then, as the angel who talked with
4 me was going away, another angel came out to meet him and said to him, Run to the young man there and tell him
5 that Jerusalem shall be a city without walls, so numerous shall be the men and cattle within it. I will be a wall of fire round her, says the LORD, and a glory in the midst of her.

6 Away, away; flee from the land of the north, says the LORD, for I will make you spread your wings like the four
7 winds of heaven, says the LORD. Away, escape, you people of Zion who live in Babylon.

8 For these are the words of the LORD of Hosts, spoken

when he sent me on a glorious mission*a* to the nations
who have plundered you, for whoever touches you
touches the apple of his eye: I raise*b* my hand against 9
them; they shall be plunder for their own slaves. So you
shall know that the LORD of Hosts has sent me. Shout 10
aloud and rejoice, daughter of Zion; I am coming, I will
make my dwelling among you, says the LORD. Many 11
nations shall come over to the LORD on that day and
become his people, and he*c* will make his dwelling with
you. Then you shall know that the LORD of Hosts has
sent me to you. The LORD will once again claim Judah as 12
his own possession in the holy land, and make Jerusalem
the city of his choice.

Silence, all mankind, in the presence of the LORD! For 13
he has bestirred himself out of his holy dwelling-place.

\* The third vision is described in verses 1–5 and is followed
by a number of oracles on the theme of the restoration of
Jerusalem.

1. *a man carrying a measuring-line:* a different word from that
in 1: 16 is used. The idea is more of a line delineating an area
than of a line used for rebuilding.

2. *To measure Jerusalem:* many commentators have assumed
from verses 4–5 that this is a reference to an early attempt to
rebuild the walls of the city. It is thought to show that the
absence of proper defences was one of the reasons given for
saying that it was not yet time to rebuild the temple (Hag.
1: 2). The building of the walls is not explicitly mentioned
here, however. The emphasis appears to be on not setting
limits to the restored city.

4. *Run to the young man there:* the identity of the young man

[*a*] on a glorious mission: *prob. rdg.; Heb.* after glory.   [*b*] *Or* wave.
[*c*] his...he: *so Pesh.; Heb.* my...I; *or, with Sept.,* his...they.

is unimportant for the meaning of the vision, but his youth may suggest inexperience in the ways of God. *Jerusalem shall be a city without walls:* the emphasis is on the unlimited size of the city. It would be wrong to set limits to the measure by which God will bless her. It is very close to the thought of Second Isaiah:

'for you shall break out of your confines right and left,
your descendants shall dispossess wide regions,
and re-people cities now desolate.'　　　　　(Isa. 54: 3)

5. *I will be a wall of fire round her:* the cautious who fear that such visionary idealism will leave them undefended are reminded of how God's presence guarded their ancestors. He was like a pillar of fire as they journeyed from Egypt in the first great act of deliverance in their history (Exod. 13: 20–2), a thought taken up elsewhere in the prophetic literature: 'over every building on Mount Zion and on all her places of assembly the LORD will create a cloud of smoke by day and a bright flame of fire by night; for glory shall be spread over all as a covering and a canopy' (Isa. 4: 5–6). *and a glory in the midst of her:* as in the Isaiah passage just quoted, the thought of the protection of the divine presence, symbolized by fire, is followed by the thought of the divine glory coming to the city, that is, the visibly manifested presence of God (cp. Hag. 1: 8). Similarly the account of the measuring of Jerusalem in Ezek. 40–2 is followed by the return of 'the glory of the God of Israel' to the city (43: 1–5). This suggests a common background to the idea in the temple worship rather than direct literary dependence between these sources.

This verse marks the climax of the third vision and suggests that the rebuilding of the temple was the occasion for its utterance. It says that God's return to the temple will be the signal for the fulfilment of the kind of promises concerning Jerusalem which the prophets of the exile, Ezekiel and Second Isaiah, had spoken. It may also have been intended to encourage the builders as Haggai did (Hag. 2: 3, 6–9).

6–7. *Away, away; flee from the land of the north:* the first of a series of brief oracles consists of a call to the exiles to return from Babylon, referred to as *the land of the north* as often in the book of Jeremiah (e.g. Jer. 31: 8). Such a call, which is a very emphatic form of promise, is also found in Jeremiah (e.g. Jer. 48: 6). *I will make you spread your wings:* the N.E.B. takes this as a promise of enlargement in harmony with the message of the vision. The tense of the Hebrew verb suggests rather that it referred to the sending into exile: 'although I spread your wings...' This oracle seems to have dated originally from the time of the Babylonian exile, and the prophet placed it here because he saw it being fulfilled in the rebuilding of the temple.

8–9. *when he sent me on a glorious mission:* the Hebrew is difficult, reading 'after glory had sent me'. The word 'glory' might be a term to denote 'God'. The N.E.B. gets good sense by a very slight emendation, however. *to the nations:* must have the sense 'against the nations'. The oracle corresponds to the second vision and, again, an origin in the exile is indicated. *the apple of his eye:* cp. Deut. 32: 10 where, although a different Hebrew word is used, the thought is of God's covenant choice and care of his people. The literal meaning could be 'the gate' of the eye, and so the 'pupil', or possibly the 'baby' of the eye. It is an idiomatic equivalent to the English phrase, the 'apple' of the eye and denotes something highly prized. *So you shall know that the LORD of Hosts has sent me:* twice in this series of oracles (cp. verse 11) the prophet stresses his divine commission which will be authenticated by events. Twice more, in the oracles the same point is stressed (4: 9; 6: 15). It may be that if some of the earlier predictions spoken in the exile appeared not to have been fulfilled, some had begun to question the authenticity of the prophet's claims. Possibly even Zechariah himself, like Jeremiah, had begun to have doubts. Now, in bringing the oracles into relation with the visions, he is claiming that both visions and oracles are finding their fulfilment in the rebuilding of the temple and all that will follow its completion.

10. *Shout aloud and rejoice, daughter of Zion:* the community of the faithful is personified as the daughter of the city, just as the word for 'city' in Hebrew is feminine because it was thought of as the 'mother' of its inhabitants. They are called to celebrate in worship the presence of God again in their midst as long before their ancestors in Jerusalem had celebrated Yahweh's kingship in his 'coming' to his temple to judge the earth (e.g. Pss. 96: 13; 98: 9). This cultic call was evidently a familiar one for it occurs again in Zeph. 3: 14 and Zech. 9: 9. It appears to be based on such passages in the Psalms as 48: 11 and 9: 14, where the Hebrew reads literally

'that I may repeat all thy praise
and exult in thy deliverance in the gates of the daughter
of Zion'

In general, in this first of a series of brief oracular sayings in verses 10-13 concerning the promises to Jerusalem, the prophet announces that the hopes expressed in the worship of the first temple are to be fulfilled in the era of the new one.

11. *Many nations shall come over to the LORD:* God's presence will make Jerusalem the centre of the pilgrimage of the nations and the place of their enlightenment (cp. Isa. 2: 2-4 = Mic. 4: 1-3). The Hebrew verb contains the note of conversion suggested by the N.E.B. This does not conflict with the threats against the nations in visions and oracles. The nations condemned are the oppressors. For the idea of even the oppressor nations coming to acknowledge Yahweh, see Ps. 2: 10-12.

12. *The LORD will once again claim Judah:* his presence in the temple will make holy the city, Judah, and the whole land. There is no real conflict with the wider outlook of verse 11. Jerusalem is to be the place where the knowledge of

God is mediated to the nations, a thought also expressed in the New Testament (Luke 24: 47).

13. *Silence, all mankind...!:* the coming of Yahweh to his people in Jerusalem will have consequences for the whole world, for he comes as king and judge (e.g. Ps. 50: 1-6). The cry for silence evidently had its origin in the cult, for it occurs elsewhere in a very similar form, cp. Hab. 2: 20; Zeph. 1: 7.  *

### THE ORDER OF CHS. 3 AND 4 IN THE N.E.B.

* The N.E.B. has introduced a number of rearrangements of the text in the book of Zechariah, of which the first occurs in chs. 3-4.

The fifth vision (in the order of the Hebrew Bible) of the lamp-stand with two olive-trees beside it is recorded in 4: 1-3, and has its explanation in 4: 11-14 (or 10*b*-14). Three passages in 4: 4-10 interrupt the vision in 4: 1-3 and its explanation. The first, 4: 4-5, consists of question and answer by which the prophet asks the angel the meaning of what he has seen. The second, in 4: 6-10*a*, is a series of short oracular sayings concerning Zerubbabel and the rebuilding of the temple. The third, in 4: 10*b*, consists of a saying about 'seven eyes'. Trying to deal with this intrusive section in ch. 4 has led to the following alterations of order in the N.E.B.:

(a) The vision of the lamp-stand and olive-trees in 4: 1-3 has been brought together with its interpretation in 4: 11-14.

(b) The question and answer of 4: 4-5 has been taken to refer, not to the vision of the lamp-stand and olive-trees, but to the fourth vision relating to Joshua in ch. 3.

(c) The reference in 4: 10*b* to 'seven eyes' has been taken to refer, not to the lamp-stand, but to the stone set before Joshua in ch. 3 (3: 9*a*), and this has been seen as the answer to the question about the meaning of what the prophet has seen, in 4: 4-5.

(d) To make this connection, the fourth vision relating to

Joshua in ch. 3 has been placed after the fifth vision of ch. 4 of the lamp-stand and two olive-trees, 3: 9a having been taken out of its place and joined with 4: 4-5 and 4: 10b.

(e) The oracular material, addressed to Zerubbabel, in 4: 6-10a, has been placed after both visions, as being not directly related to either.

In favour of such rearrangement of the text it can be said that the text obviously had become out of order, especially with the insertion of 4: 6-10a between 4: 1-3 and 4: 11-14 (or 10b-14, if the reference to the seven eyes did originally refer to the lamp-stand). Again, this does establish some kind of logical order. Against it can be alleged that it imposes one of a number of possible interpretations on the text. It obscures any exegetical purpose there may have been behind the order of the text, whether the prophet or another was responsible for that order. ✣


FOURTH (FIFTH) VISION – GOD'S PRESENCE IN HIS
TEMPLE

4 1[a] The angel who talked with me came back and roused me as a man is roused from sleep. He asked me what I
2 saw, and I answered, 'A lamp-stand all of gold with a bowl on it; it holds seven lamps, and there are seven
3 pipes[b] for the lamps on top of it, with two olive-trees standing by it, one on the right of the bowl and another
11[c] on the left.' I asked him, 'What are these two olive-trees, the one on the right and the other on the left of the lamp-
12 stand?' I asked also another question, 'What are the two sprays of olive beside the golden pipes which discharge

[a] 3: 1-10 transposed to follow 4: 14.
[b] seven pipes: so Sept.; Heb. seven pipes each.
[c] 4: 4-10 transposed to follow 3: 10.

the golden oil from their bowls[a]?' He said, 'Do you not 13
know what these mean?' 'No, sir', I answered. 'These 14
two', he said, 'are the two consecrated with oil[b] who
attend the Lord of all the earth.'

☆ 2. *A lamp-stand all of gold. . . :* the description of the lamp-
stand is obscure. It probably represents a central bowl as a
reservoir of oil, around which are grouped seven lamps, each
connected to the bowl by a pipe. The Hebrew, 'seven pipes
for each lamp' even suggests seven clusters of seven lamps,
making forty-nine in all! It was probably suggested by the
single great lamp in the second temple referred to in 1 Macc.
1: 21, although this appears to have been a straight, seven-
branched lamp. It represented the presence of God in the
midst of his people and is so understood in verse 14. If, in
spite of the N.E.B., the question and answer of 4: 4–5 and 10*b*
do belong to this vision, then it suggests also God's watchful-
ness from the temple over the fortunes of all his people. This
would suggest a time of origin for the vision after the temple
had been completed, expressing the conviction that its completion had significance not only for the faithful in Jerusalem
and Judah, but for the Jews living in dispersion in other
countries as well. These are usually referred to as 'The
Diaspora' or 'The Dispersion'. The N.E.B., however, takes
these verses in connection with the seven-faceted stone set
before Joshua in the fourth vision of ch. 3.

12. *I asked also another question:* this question and its answer
looks like a later, secondary insertion into the text. It is asked
before the reply to the previous question has been given. It
also introduces additional features not mentioned in the vision.
It refers to the two leaders as 'branches', and the Hebrew text
suggests that they were supplying the lamp with oil. Since
they would hardly be supplying God with strength, this must
represent a secondary interpretation of one detail of the vision.

[a] their bowls: *lit.* upon them.          [b] *Lit.* two sons of oil.

It is an interpretation which suggests an even more 'sacral' view of the office of governor and high priest than that of verse 14, which represents an earlier development of the text than verse 12. Here the leaders are seen as mediators of the divine life and blessing to the community. It is thus much closer to the outlook of the editor of the book of Haggai, with his emphasis on the role of the leaders. Like him, it makes no real distinction between them in status or in function.

14. '*These two...are the two consecrated with oil who attend the Lord of all the earth*': this probably represents the first explanation of the significance of the two olive-trees. It shows Zerubbabel and Joshua simply as 'standing by' or 'attending' God. *consecrated with oil* refers to their anointing as civil governor and high priest respectively. It emphasizes that they receive their authority and power to govern from God and act primarily as his servants. If, as seems possible, the main emphasis of this vision was intended to be on the presence of God in the temple, then this represented an extension of its original meaning at a stage when the role of the leadership was beginning to become an issue. The use of the word *Lord* for God where Zechariah always uses Yahweh (LORD, see p. 15) strengthens this impression. The civil governor has only a 'sacral' role within the temple, no political or military one, and the high priest is his equal. Such a view rests on seeing 4: 4–5 and 10*b* as part of the original vision, however. If the N.E.B. is right in transferring the questions and answer of these verses to the fourth vision in ch. 3, then the emphasis of the fifth vision in ch. 4 was on the leaders from the first.  ✻

FIFTH (FOURTH) VISION – THE CLEANSING AND CROWNING OF THE HIGH PRIEST

**3** 1 Then he showed me Joshua the high priest standing before the angel of the LORD, with the Adversary[a] stand-

[a] *Heb.* the Satan.

ing at his right hand to accuse him. The LORD said to the 2
Adversary, 'The LORD rebuke you, Satan, the LORD
rebuke you who are venting your spite on Jerusalem.*ᵃ* Is
not this man a brand snatched from the fire?' Now 3
Joshua was wearing filthy clothes as he stood before the 4
angel; and the angel turned and said to those in attendance
on him, 'Take off his filthy clothes.' Then he turned to
him and said, 'See how I have taken away your guilt from
you; I will clothe you in fine vestments'; and he*ᵇ* added,
'Let a clean turban be put on his head.' So they put a clean 5
turban on his head and clothed him in clean*ᶜ* garments,
while the angel of the LORD stood by. Then the angel of 6
the LORD gave Joshua this solemn charge: These are the 7
words of the LORD of Hosts: If you will conform to my
ways and carry out your duties, you shall administer my
house and be in control of my courts, and I grant you the
right to come and go amongst these in attendance here.
Listen, Joshua the high priest, you and your colleagues 8
seated here before you, all you who are an omen of
things to come: I will now bring my servant, the Branch.
In one day I will wipe away the guilt of the land. On that 9–10
day, says the LORD of Hosts, you shall all of you invite
one another to come and sit each under his vine and his
fig-tree.

\* There are a number of unique features about this vision.
The usual introductory formula is missing; there is no inquiry
about the meaning of the vision from an interpreting angel.
Rather, the scene and its meaning unfold independently of

[a] the LORD . . . Jerusalem: *or* the LORD who has chosen Jerusalem rebuke
you.      [b] *So Pesh.; Heb.* I.
[c] clean: *prob. rdg., cp. Pesh.; Heb. om.*

the prophet with no question and answer. This has led a number of commentators to question whether it was added later to an original series of seven visions. A decision on this depends on content as well as form.

1. *Then he showed me Joshua the high priest standing before the angel of the LORD:* the vision, in which the high priest alone is the central figure, takes place in heaven where the Council of Heaven (see p. 15) is presided over by God and his angel. *with the Adversary standing...to accuse him:* the Hebrew word for *Adversary* is 'Satan', but with the definite article before it, it denotes an office rather than a personal name. As in Job 1–2 he is the figure in the Council of Heaven who has the role of Counsel for the Prosecution. The nature of the accusation is not specified but there are strong suggestions that Joshua here is the representative of the community returned from the disgrace of the exile.

2. *The LORD rebuke you, Satan:* by an act of divine mercy the guilt and distress of the exile are set aside. *who are venting your spite on Jerusalem:* the translators of the N.E.B. have not disclosed their reasons for choosing this rendering. The footnote is certainly to be preferred, 'the LORD who has chosen Jerusalem rebuke you'. God's mercy to Joshua and the community he represents is based on his divine election of Jerusalem, that is his choice of Jerusalem as the place where he makes his presence known. *a brand snatched from the fire:* a phrase which occurs also in Amos 4: 11. The reference is to the return of Joshua and the people from exile by an act of divine grace.

3. *Now Joshua was wearing filthy clothes:* such clothes could be a sign of mourning and distress (e.g. Jer. 41: 4–5), but are more probably a sign of guilt and contamination from Babylon. The passage seems to be based on the instructions for installing a priest, described in Lev. 8: 1–9. Joshua needs an act of divine installation if he is to be fit to act as high priest after the shame of the exile.

5. *and he added, 'Let a clean turban be put on his head':* the

Hebrew has, 'And I said...', representing the sole inter-
ruption of the prophet in the scene. This may be to emphasize
the crowning with the turban as the climax. It has been shown
that this resembles the crowning ceremony for Babylonian
kings. Others have argued that the Israelite kings were also
reinstalled each year in Jerusalem after an act of ritual humili-
ation at the New Year Festival. The Hebrew word for
'turban', however, is neither that for the king's crown nor
the high priest's turban in Lev. 8. It is used elsewhere only in
a symbolic sense, as in Job 29: 14 and, interestingly, in a later
prophetic text of promise to the restored community:

'you will be a glorious crown in the LORD's hand,
    a kingly diadem (turban) in the hand of your God.'
                                        (Isa. 62: 3)

6. *Then the angel of the LORD gave Joshua this solemn charge:*
the oracles addressed to Joshua in verses 6–10 may be secondary
to the vision as such, but the fact that the vision concentrates
solely on the installation of Joshua as high priest suggests that
the whole had belonged together from an early stage of its
transmission. The significant fact is that the privileges granted
to Joshua, namely administration of the temple and its
precincts and the role of intermediary between God and the
community, all belonged to the king before the exile.

8. *all you who are an omen of things to come:* the same phrase
is used of Isaiah and his disciples (Isa. 8: 16–18), only they
were omens of judgement. The high priest and his colleagues
(and successors?) are omens of God's blessing to come upon
the community. *I will now bring my servant, the Branch:* the
term *Branch* has messianic significance in the prophetic
literature:

'Then a shoot shall grow from the stock of Jesse,
    and a branch shall spring from his roots.'
                                        (Isa. 11: 1)

'The days are now coming, says the LORD,
    when I will make a righteous Branch spring from
        David's line,
    a king who shall rule wisely'

(Jer. 23: 5; cp. 33: 15)

In Zech. 3: 8 the Branch is not named as Zerubbabel, and his coming is entirely dependent on the faithfulness of the priestly line. This does not fit the picture of Joshua and Zerubbabel co-operating together at the time of the rebuilding of the temple. One possible explanation would be that this vision originated from an earlier period in the prophet's ministry before the temple reconstruction had begun. We should have to assume that Joshua had returned to Jerusalem before Zerubbabel. On the other hand this could be a later oracle, reflecting the growth of the priesthood in power and influence at the expense of the role of the civil governor at a time when it was believed that the priesthood had taken over entirely the royal privileges and responsibilities. Meanwhile, its continuing ministry is a guarantee that in a future time of salvation the promised messianic ruler will come. Such a messianic figure could still be seen as an ideal descendant of David. It is interesting that in later Jewish literature there is testimony to the expectation of the joint rule of two Messiahs, one a priestly figure and the other a descendant of the royal house of David (e.g. *The Testament of Levi*, 18). If this second interpretation is correct (and see the comments on 6: 9–15), it would strongly suggest that the vision and its oracles were a later addition to an original series of seven, reflecting the process by which the priests came to sole prominence in the community after the exile.

10. *and sit each under his vine and his fig-tree:* a traditional picture of peace and prosperity in the time of salvation (cp. Mic. 4: 4). It recalls the traditions of the ideal conditions of Solomon's reign (1 Kings 4: 25). ✻

### PROMISES CONCERNING JOSHUA AND ZERUBBABEL

Here is the stone that I set before Joshua, a stone in which are seven eyes. I will reveal its meaning to you, says the LORD of Hosts. Then I asked the angel of the **4** 4*a* LORD who talked with me, 'Sir, what are these?' And he answered, 'Do you not know what these mean?' 'No, 5 sir', I answered. 'These seven', he said, 'are the eyes of the LORD ranging over the whole earth.'*b*

Then he turned and said to me, This is the word of the 6 LORD concerning Zerubbabel: Neither by force of arms nor by brute strength, but by my spirit! says the LORD of Hosts. How does a mountain, the greatest mountain, 7 compare with Zerubbabel? It is no higher than a plain. He shall bring out the stone called Possession*cd* while men acclaim its beauty. This word came to me from the 8, 9 LORD: Zerubbabel with his own hands laid the foundation of this house and with his own hands he shall finish it. So shall you know that the LORD of Hosts has sent me to you. Who has despised the day of small things? He shall 10 rejoice when he sees Zerubbabel holding the stone called Separation.*d*

✻ 3: 9*a*. *Here is the stone that I set before Joshua . . . :* as stated in the note on the order of the text (see pp. 45–6) this verse has been detached in the N.E.B. from its place in ch. 3; it is followed by the question and answer of 4: 4–5 which the order of the Hebrew Bible associates with the vision of the lamp-stand, and it has all been brought into connection with 4: 10*b*, which

[*a*] *See note on 4: 11 above.*
[*b*] These seven . . . earth: *transposed from verse 10.*
[*c*] *So Sept.; Heb.* Top.    [*d*] *Cp. Lev. 20: 24–6.*

is taken to refer to this stone set before Joshua. It is not clear
what the stone is. Some have seen it as a stone in the temple,
headstone or foundation stone, as in 4: 7. If, as the N.E.B.
suggests, it is linked with 4: 10*b*, that is, with 'the eyes of the
LORD ranging over the whole earth', then it might well be
suggesting God's watchful presence in his temple. But why
should it then be set before Joshua rather than Zerubbabel?
Others take it to be a reference to the gold rosette set in the
high priest's turban (Exod. 28: 36–9) which is clearly said to
have had expiatory significance. If it belongs with 3: 9*b*,
which speaks of God removing the guilt of the land in a
single day (and this is where it is placed in the Hebrew Bible),
then it is given a similar significance here. The rosette was
inscribed 'Holiness to the LORD', seven characters in Hebrew,
which some take to explain the seven eyes. Whatever the
import of the stone, it is clearly the high priest's role in
mediating the blessing of God to the community which is
being stressed. *I will reveal its meaning to you:* the N.E.B. has
taken the meaning of the Hebrew verb, usually translated
'to engrave', as 'to loose' and hence 'to explain' the inscription on the stone. The verb does mean 'to loose' but is
not used in this metaphorical sense elsewhere in the Old
Testament.

6. *Neither by force of arms...but by my spirit!:* only in 7: 12
is the spirit of God referred to in Zech. 1–8. Elsewhere the
emphasis is on the direct and immediate activity of God.
There is also a reference to the spirit of God in the expanded
material of the book of Haggai (2: 5). This raises the possibility that this brief series of oracles also springs from the
tradition rather than directly from the prophet. While
Zechariah would have spoken about the role of Zerubbabel
in building the temple, the material is intrusive where it
appears. However, the reference in 4: 14 to the 'two consecrated with oil', i.e. the 'anointed ones', would give reason
for the insertion of a reference to the spirit of God there in
ch. 4, where it appears in the Hebrew text. This saying is not

only a clear rejection of all military means by which the civil governor might seek to establish God's rule, but also a very clear limitation of his role to a purely cultic sphere. These oracles in verses 6–10 limit Zerubbabel's role entirely to building the temple in which, it has already been claimed, the priest exercises sole and absolute rights. The form and position of this brief series of oracles in the Hebrew Bible, therefore, mean that, like the material in 3, it may have belonged to a stage in the development of the tradition when the priesthood was coming into prominence in place of a civil governor.

7. *How does a mountain...compare with Zerubbabel?:* probably the reference is metaphorical rather than a literal description of the 'mountains' of rubble. Zerubbabel, empowered by the 'spirit', will prove equal to all the obstacles in the way of rebuilding. *the stone called Possession:* the Hebrew has 'headstone', which might refer either to the foundation stone or the final stone laid on the pinnacle of the completed building. The N.E.B. here follows the attractive Septuagint reading which sees the completion of the temple as marking out the community as God's own people.

9. *So shall you know that the LORD of Hosts has sent me to you:* the main aim of Zechariah, as with Haggai, was to encourage the people to build the temple. In its completion, and in the experience of all the blessings which would flow to the community as a result, the mission of the prophet would find its vindication.

10. *Who has despised the day of small things?:* an oracle of encouragement akin to that of Hag. 2: 3. If the present form of this series of oracles is due to the editor, he may well have seen them as a word to the people of his own day who saw the temple completed but with only small signs of the promised consequences. *the stone called Separation:* a phrase which has puzzled commentators. Some have seen it as a plummet made of a mixture (i.e. a 'separation') of metal alloys. Others have seen a reference to some unknown

technical building term, or a stone set aside for its special
beauty for use as a headstone. The N.E.B. has followed the
Syriac Version. The stone which marks the completion of the
temple, which designates the community as God's own
'possession', also shows them to be a people 'separated' to
him for his service: 'I have made a clear separation between
you and the heathen, that you may belong to me' (Lev.
20: 26). The implication is that they are to live in obedience
to God's demands and so be 'separate' from other people.
While Zechariah himself may have stressed the need for such
'separation' it may well have been of special relevance for
those among whom the tradition was handed down in
times of greater pressure on the faith and practice of Judaism. *

### SIXTH AND SEVENTH VISIONS – THE CLEANSING
### OF THE COMMUNITY

5 1, 2  I looked up again and saw a flying scroll. He asked me
what I saw, and I answered, 'A flying scroll, twenty
3 cubits long and ten cubits wide.' This, he told me, is the
curse which goes out over the whole land; for by the
writing on one side every thief shall be swept clean away,
and by the writing on the other every perjurer shall be
4 swept clean away. I have sent it out, the LORD of Hosts
has said, and it shall enter the house of the thief and the
house of the man who has perjured himself in my name;
it shall stay inside that house and demolish it, timbers and
stones and all.

5  The angel who talked with me came out and said to
me, 'Raise your eyes and look at this thing that comes
6 forth.' I asked what it was, and he said, 'It is a great
barrel[a] coming forth,' and he added, 'so great is their

[a] a great barrel: *Heb.* an ephah.

guilt[a] in all the land.' Then a round slab of lead was lifted, 7
and a woman was sitting there inside the barrel. He said, 8
'This is Wickedness', and he thrust her down into the
barrel and rammed the leaden weight upon its mouth.
I looked up again and saw two women coming forth with 9
the wind in their wings (for they had wings like a stork's),
and they carried the barrel between earth and sky. I asked 10
the angel who talked with me where they were taking
the barrel, and he answered, 'To build a house for it[b] in 11
the land of Shinar; when the house is ready, it[c] shall be
set on the place prepared for it[b] there.'

* 2. *A flying scroll, twenty cubits long and ten cubits wide:* the
books of Jeremiah (Jer. 36: 2) and Ezekiel (Ezek. 2: 9; 3: 1–3)
had spoken of 'scrolls' which contained God's message of
judgement. They were both prophets who had stressed that
God would judge each individual for his sin rather than the
community as a whole (Jer. 31: 29–30; Ezek. 18: 1–4), just as
the message of this vision in Zechariah is that individual
sinners will be rooted out of the community (verse 4).
Ezekiel's scroll, like this one, was written on both sides (Ezek.
2: 10; cp. Zech. 5: 3). The measurements of the scroll correspond exactly to the dimensions of the porch in Solomon's
temple (1 Kings 6: 3), perhaps signifying that God's judgement
would go out from the completed temple where he dwelt
among his people.

3. *This...is the curse which goes out over the whole land:* the
word for *curse* is that which in Deuteronomy speaks of God's
judgement against the individual who breaks the terms of the
covenant (Deut. 29: 21). Once God is present in the temple
the covenant will be renewed again and the holy land
cleansed of defilement by the sin of the covenant-breakers.

6. *It is a great barrel:* the Hebrew word is 'Ephah', denoting

[a] guilt: *so Sept.; Heb.* eye.      [b] *Or* her.      [c] *Or* she.

a large container named after the amount it held. This would be roughly equivalent to 5 gallons (about 23 litres) but in such a visionary passage the size has no literal significance. *so great is their guilt:* the N.E.B. rightly follows the Septuagint here (see footnote).

8. *'This is Wickedness':* ancient myths provide a number of variations on the idea of a wicked genie 'bottled up' in a jar, but the thought of the land being cleansed from wickedness, personified as a woman, is close to Ezek. 36: 17: 'when the house of Israel dwelt in their own land, they defiled it by their ways and their doings; their conduct before me was like the uncleanness of a woman in her impurity' (Revised Standard Version).

9. *two women...(for they had wings like a stork's):* the two women apparently have no allegorical significance, but it is interesting that the Hebrew word for *stork* is closely related to the word for 'devoted', 'faithful'. Did a later commentator wish to suggest that the loyal and devoted among the community had a 'cleansing' effect? If so, the note must be secondary since, for the prophet, all the emphasis is on God's powerful and gracious act of cleansing.

11. *To build a house for it:* the Hebrew word for *house* also means 'temple' and suggests that, where the sixth vision spoke of the cleansing of the community from social sins, the seventh speaks of the removal of all false and idolatrous worship. *in the land of Shinar:* the archaic name for Babylon, found in Gen. 11: 2 in the story of the tower of Babel. There is irony in the suggestion that idolatry is relegated to Babylon – the only place fit for it.

The two visions of ch. 5 together form a picture of the divine cleansing and renewal of the community. They would fit well in the time when the prophet saw the temple building nearing completion. They express his hopes, which rose with the building. ✳

## EIGHTH VISION – GOD'S WILL ACCOMPLISHED
### THROUGHOUT THE EARTH

I looked up again and saw four chariots coming out **6**
between two mountains, and the mountains were made 2
of copper.[a] The first chariot had bay horses, the second 3
black, the third white, and the fourth dappled.[b] I asked 4
the angel who talked with me, 'Sir, what are these?' He 5
answered, 'These are the four winds of heaven which
have been attending the Lord of the whole earth, and
they are now going forth. The chariot with the black 6
horses is going to the land of the north, that with the
white to the far west,[c] that with the dappled to the south,
and that with the roan to the land of the east.'[d] They were 7
eager to go and range over the whole earth; so he said,
'Go and range over the earth', and the chariots did so.
Then he called me to look and said, 'Those going to the 8
land of the north have given my spirit rest in the land of
the north.'

✴ 1. *I...saw four chariots:* this last vision has certain parallels
to the first, although only horsemen were mentioned there.
*coming out between two mountains, and the mountains were made
of copper:* in Babylonian mythology the sun god was believed
to rise from between two mountains. Perhaps there was
influence closer at hand, however, for in the porch of Solomon's temple were two bronze pillars called Jachin and Boaz
(1 Kings 7: 13–22). The names may have meant 'It shall
stand' and 'In strength' (see the N.E.B. footnote to 1 Kings
7: 21), and thus denoted strength and power. They may have

[a] Or bronze.  [b] *Prob. rdg., cp. Sept.; Heb.* adds roan.
[c] to the far west: *prob. rdg.; Heb.* behind them.
[d] to the land of the east: *prob. rdg.; Heb. om.*

suggested to the prophet the idea of God holding sway over the four corners of the earth from the rebuilt temple.

5. *These are the four winds of heaven:* some have wanted to read 'like' *the four winds of heaven* since, if the chariots are already metaphors of the messengers of God, this adds metaphor to metaphor. Others have wanted to read 'to' *the four winds of heaven.* The details are unimportant. What is being stressed is God's universal sovereignty.

6. *to the land of the north:* Zechariah's way of describing Babylon (cp. 2: 6–7). This is perhaps because in Canaanite mythology the mountain where the gods dwelt was situated in 'the far north' and in prophetic literature it had been the direction from which traditionally the enemies of God's people came (e.g. Jer. 6: 1). *that with the white to the far west:* this rests on a very slight emendation of the Hebrew text which reads, 'and the white horses after them'. Slight as the emendation is, however, it may not be necessary. Verse 8 shows that all the original emphasis of the vision was on what happened 'in the land of the north'. It may be, therefore, that originally both black and white horses were spoken of as going there. This would have symbolized dark judgement for the Babylonians and bright deliverance for the Jewish exiles. Indeed, some discrepancies between the colour of the horses in verses 2–3 and 6, and the omission in verse 6 of any reference to horses going to the east, may indicate that the detailed emphasis on the colour of the horses and their journeys to all parts of the earth are secondary. In a later time, when there was a large Jewish Diaspora not only in Babylon but in many parts of the world, the hope of the vision was extended to them. The number four in the original vision, signifying God's world-wide dominion, would have lent itself to such particularizing.

8. *have given my spirit rest:* there is a difference between this and the 'rest' of the first vision which provoked the cry 'How long, O LORD?' It is as though we have been brought to the last act of a play in which all the tensions and conflicts have

been resolved. Now there is peace, not the peace of helpless suffering, but peace because of God's universal sway. Babylon has been judged and the exiles liberated. We cannot tell at what stage of Zechariah's ministry this would first have been uttered. If originally it belonged to the time of the return from exile, it has been fittingly placed here as the climax of the visions, expressing the confidence of the prophet as the temple neared completion. God's subjugation of Babylon and bringing home of many exiles are only a foretaste of the complete and world-wide victory which is to come.  ✻

### THE SYMBOLIC CROWNING

The word of the LORD came to me: Take silver and 9, 10 gold from the exiles, from Heldai, Tobiah, Jedaiah, and*a* Josiah son of Zephaniah, who have come back from Babylon. Take it and make a crown;*b* put the crown on 11 the head of Joshua son of Jehozadak, the high priest,*c* and 12 say to him, These are the words of the LORD of Hosts: Here is a man named the Branch; he will shoot up from the ground where he is and will build the temple of the LORD. It is he who will build the temple of the LORD, he 13 who will assume royal dignity, will be seated on his throne and govern, with a priest at his right side,*d* and concord shall prevail between them. The crown shall be 14 in the charge of Heldai,*e* Tobiah, Jedaiah, and Josiah*f* son of Zephaniah, as a memorial in the temple of the LORD.

[a] and: *prob. rdg.; Heb.* and go on that day yourself and go to the house of...     [b] *So Pesh.; Heb.* crowns.
[c] Joshua...priest: *possibly an error for* Zerubbabel son of Shealtiel, *cp. 3: 5; 4: 9.*     [d] at...side: *so Sept.; Heb.* on his throne.
[e] *So Pesh.; Heb.* Helem.     [f] *So Pesh.; Heb.* favour.

15     Men from far away shall come and work on the building of the temple of the LORD; so shall you know that the LORD of Hosts has sent me to you. If only you will obey the LORD your God!

✴ 10. *Take silver and gold from the exiles:* nothing is known of those named. Indeed, differences between the names in verses 10 and 14 (see the N.E.B. footnotes) suggest that the lists were secondary, and perhaps altered in the course of transmission. The thought of exiles contributing with Jews at home to the building-up of the temple fits well with the last vision with its thought of God at work in Babylon, and shows why verses 9–15 were added at this point. It would also have brought assurance to the Jews of the Diaspora at a later time when that Diaspora was larger and spread farther afield. It would have assured them that they too belonged to the cultic community with Jews at home, and were being urged to play their part in support of, and allegiance to, the temple, its worship and its community.

11. *Take it and make a crown:* much has been made of the fact that the word in Hebrew is plural, 'crowns', and yet only the crowning of Joshua is mentioned. However, elsewhere the same Hebrew word appears in a plural form where it clearly refers to only one crown (Job 31: 36). The plural form may be used because such a crown had a number of bands. It is unlikely that the text at one time intended to suggest two crowns, one for Zerubbabel and one for Joshua. *put the crown on the head of Joshua...the high priest:* it has been found strange that Joshua is spoken of as being crowned, while what follows appears to refer to a messianic ruler. We cannot assume that political troubles led the Persians to remove Zerubbabel from office, following which the text was altered to speak of Joshua only. It is possible that Joshua was crowned symbolically on Zerubbabel's behalf before the civil governor had come from Babylon. However, the following points should be noted:

(a) Again, as in the 'messianic' reference of 3 : 8, the 'Branch' is not identified by name with Zerubbabel.

(b) As in 3 : 8 the priestly line is seen as being the guarantee of the coming of the messianic ruler of the future.

(c) The priests meanwhile do exercise the rule; cp. the crowning of Joshua alone here with 3 : 7.

(d) Even in the future when the messianic ruler has come, a joint rule with the priestly line is envisaged.

(e) Verse 14 suggests that the continuing rule of the priests in the temple is a 'reminder' of God's promises for the community's future.

(f) The call to put the crown in the temple, as a 'reminder' or 'memorial' of the coming Branch, suggests a time later than Zerubbabel's return from Babylon. By the time a temple was there in which to put the crown, he had returned and done his work.

All this makes it likely that the nucleus of an original oracle by Zechariah predicting that Zerubbabel would build the temple (perhaps simply verse 13; cp. 4: 6–10*a*) has been taken and moulded in the tradition to fit what actually happened afterwards. It was the priestly line which came to the fore and they were seen as divinely appointed rulers of the community and administrators of the temple, guarantees of a future messianic ruler who would 'build' the temple in the sense of 'building up the community of God's faithful people'. Such a view of 6: 9–15 corresponds exactly to the picture we get from 3: 8 (see commentary pp. 51–2) and confirms the impression that that also relates, not to a time before Zerubbabel's return to Jerusalem, but to the later situation of those who passed on the tradition.

15. *Men from far away shall come and work on the building of the temple of the LORD:* with verses 9–10 this is an assurance to faithful Jews scattered throughout the world that they also belong to the community of the temple and will inherit with those at home the future salvation Zechariah had promised. *so shall you know . . . :* the divine authentication of Zechariah's

mission, which the prophet himself had claimed would be in the completion of the temple, is now taken farther into the future. It will be vindicated when all that the prophet foretold came to pass. *If only you will obey the LORD your God!:* a call to the continuing community to be faithful, so proving worthy of the future age and hastening its day. It is close to the spirit of Deut. 28: 1–2: 'and all these blessings shall come to you...because you obey the LORD your God'.

So in 6: 9–15 the visions of Zechariah which he related to the completion of the temple in 515 B.C. are cast into the future and made applicable, with both their comfort and their challenge, to the editor's own generation. ✷

# *Joy and gladness in the coming age*

### WORSHIP IS TO EXPRESS A NEW WAY OF LIFE

7 THE WORD OF THE LORD came to Zechariah in the fourth year of the reign of King Darius, on the fourth
2 day of Kislev, the ninth month. Bethel-sharezer sent Regem-melech with his men to seek the favour of the
3 LORD. They were to say to the priests in the house of the LORD of Hosts and to the prophets, 'Am I to lament and abstain in the fifth month as I have done for so many
4 years?' Then the word of the LORD of Hosts came to me:
5 Say to all the people of the land and to the priests, When you fasted and lamented in the fifth and seventh months these seventy years, was it indeed in my honour that you
6 fasted? And when you ate and drank, was it not to please
7 yourselves? Was it not this that the LORD proclaimed

through the prophets of old, while Jerusalem was populous and peaceful, as were the cities round her, and the Negeb and the Shephelah?

The word of the LORD came to Zechariah: These are 8, 9 the words of the LORD of Hosts: Administer true justice, show loyalty and compassion to one another, do not oppress the orphan and the widow, the alien and the poor, 10 do not contrive any evil one against another. But they 11 refused to listen, they turned their backs on me in defiance, they stopped their ears and would not hear. Their hearts 12 were adamant; they refused to accept instruction and all that the LORD of Hosts had taught them by his spirit through the prophets of old; and they suffered under the anger of the LORD of Hosts. As they did not listen when 13 I[a] called, so I did not listen when they called, says the 14 LORD of Hosts, and I drove them out among all the nations to whom they were strangers, leaving their land a waste behind them, so that no one came and went. Thus they made their pleasant land a waste.

✶ 1. *in the fourth year of the reign of King Darius:* 518 B.C. *Kislev, the ninth month:* November/December, a little under two years later than the date given for the visions.

2. *Bethel-sharezer sent Regem-melech with his men...:* the Hebrew can be interpreted in a number of ways:
(a) 'Bethel sent Sharezer, Regem-melech and his men...': taken in this way it means that the people, or perhaps the priests of Bethel are the subject of the action in sending the inquiry. Some who interpret it in this way see what follows in verses 5–7 as an answer by the prophet rejecting their worship altogether in Bethel. Some think this reflects Jewish attitudes to the worship of the Samaritans.

[a] *Prob. rdg.; Heb.* he.

(b) 'He' (subject unspecified) or 'Sharezer sent to Bethel...':
it seems unlikely that such an inquiry should be directed to
the sanctuary at Bethel, but that is how all the Versions read it.
(c) It can be taken as the N.E.B. has taken it with Bethel-
sharezer seen as a proper name. Similar names are found elsewhere in the Old Testament (e.g. Jer. 39: 3). Of these possible
interpretations this is the most likely. *Regem-melech* could be a
personal name or the title of an office, 'chief officer of the
king'. It could even be in apposition to the name and be
rendered, 'Bethel-sharezer, the chief officer of the king,
sent...' We do not know who Bethel-sharezer could have
been. It is a Babylonian name, so he could be either a Jew in
exile there who had achieved some position and who acted
on behalf of the Jewish community, or a successor to Zerubbabel as governor or possibly a gentile proselyte, that is, a
convert to the Jewish faith.

3. *to the priests in the house of the LORD of Hosts and to the
prophets:* the two appear to have functioned alongside each
other in the temple after the exile as they had done before
(cp. Mic. 3: 11). This verse suggests that the incident is to be
dated after the completion of the temple in spite of the date
of verse 1. That may be editorial, to distinguish the material
in chs. 7 and 8 from the visions which have preceded them.
*Am I to lament and abstain in the fifth month...?:* the fifth
month was the month in which the temple had been destroyed
(2 Kings 25: 8–9). Presumably a regular day of mourning had
marked the event annually. The point of the question seems
to be, 'Now that the temple is rebuilt should we go on fasting
and observing the destruction of the old one?' Perhaps behind
it lies a deeper question: 'Has the new age which the prophet
promised would follow the rebuilding of the temple begun or
not?' The prophet in his answer in 8: 18–19 certainly takes it
in this way. *the fifth month* does not necessarily imply a four-
month delay (verse 1). The question about the fast of the fifth
month does not need to have been asked in the fifth month.

4. *Then the word of the LORD of Hosts came to me:* this intro-

duces a number of oracles in ch. 7 which have come between the question of verse 3 and its answer in 8: 18-19. This first oracle of verses 4-7, continued in verses 11-14, has obviously been added because of its general relation to the theme of fasting.

5. *fifth and seventh months:* the mention of the fast in the seventh month (possibly observing the murder of Gedaliah, 2 Kings 25: 25) suggests that this oracle was not originally directly related to the question of verse 3. *these seventy years:* a general reference to the period of the exile (see comment on 1: 12).

5-6. *was it indeed in my honour that you fasted? And when you ate and drank, was it not to please yourselves?:* the general indict-ment is that both fasts and religious festivals have been self-centred acts not expressing an approach to God in true worship and penitence (cp. Isa. 58: 3-7).

7. *Was it not this that the LORD proclaimed through the prophets of old...?:* even during the exile they had been repeating the sins of their ancestors which had brought judge-ment upon them and which had been so strongly denounced by the earlier prophets.

8-10. *Administer true justice...:* the reference to earlier prophets has led someone to insert a short summary of their ethical teaching. It is unrelated to the theme of fasting and interrupts the sequence of verses 4-7 and 11-14, and so is clearly secondary.

11-14. *But they refused to listen...:* these verses are closely parallel to 1: 1-6 and, like that passage, share a number of points in common with the kind of hortatory, sermonic material recorded by the Chronicler (e.g. 2 Chron. 30: 6-9; Neh. 9: 25-31). This last passage shows a similar association between prophecy and the spirit of God (Neh. 9: 30) as here in verse 12. It suggests that here and in 1: 1-6 an original nucleus of Zechariah's preaching has been edited by those familiar with the kind of temple sermons the Chronicler knew and drew on. By this means, Zechariah's warnings not to

disregard the words of the earlier prophets were driven home
to the editor's own contemporaries. ✶

## BLESSINGS OF THE TIME OF SALVATION

**8** 1, 2    The word of the LORD of Hosts came to me: These are
the words of the LORD of Hosts: I have been very jealous
3 for Zion, fiercely jealous for her. Now, says the LORD, I
have come back to Zion and I will dwell in Jerusalem.
Jerusalem shall be called the City of Truth, and the mountain of the LORD of Hosts shall be called the Holy Moun-
4 tain. These are the words of the LORD of Hosts: Once
again shall old men and old women sit in the streets of
Jerusalem, each leaning on a stick because of their great
5 age; and the streets of the city shall be full of boys and
6 girls, playing in the streets. These are the words of the
LORD of Hosts: Even if it may seem impossible*a* to the
survivors of this nation on that day, will it also seem
impossible to me?*b* This is the very word of the LORD
7 of Hosts. These are the words of the LORD of Hosts: See,
8 I will rescue my people from the countries of the east and
the west, and bring them back to live in Jerusalem. They
shall be my people, and I will be their God, in truth and
justice.

✶ Ch. 8 contains a series of sayings which complete the
words of Zechariah with an assurance of the blessings of the
coming age of salvation. Verses 18-19 give his answer to the
question put by the embassy in 7: 1-3.
    1. *The word of the LORD of Hosts came to me:* the Hebrew

[a] Or wonderful.
[b] will...me?: or it will seem wonderful also to me.

lacks *to me*, making this a most unusual introductory formula. It may suggest that the words recorded in this chapter were seen as being, not to Zechariah alone, but to the editor's contemporaries.

2. *I have been very jealous for Zion:* an exact quotation of the oracle of 1: 14. The readers are thus reminded that God's concern for Jerusalem, of which Zechariah spoke, is still active.

3. *I have come back to Zion:* a quotation of the oracle in 1: 16, although here, significantly, the consequence is not the re-building of the temple, but the purification of the community. *City of Truth...Holy Mountain:* general allusions to the fulfilment of earlier prophetic promises (e.g. Isa. 1: 21-6).

4-5. *Once again shall old men and old women sit in the streets of Jerusalem....:* another oracle giving an idyllic picture of peace, longevity and increase of population, fulfilling such prophecies as Jer. 30: 18-21. It goes farther in attempting to describe the nature of the age of salvation than anything Zechariah (or Haggai) said.

6. *will it also seem impossible to me?:* the N.E.B., without giving a word-for-word translation, accurately reproduces the sense. This could have been the nucleus of an oracle of Zechariah spoken to encourage the temple builders, and now applied to the task of bringing in the age of salvation. The description of the community as the 'remnant' (N.E.B. *survivors*) follows the usage of the editor of the book of Haggai. It is not used by Zechariah in the visions or oracles directly from him. Again, the editor is assuring his readers that the community in Jerusalem, whatever they may be undergoing, are to inherit the blessings proclaimed by the prophets to the 'remnant'. *

JUDGEMENT REVERSED

These are the words of the LORD of Hosts: Take cour- 9 age, you who in these days hear, from the prophets who were present when the foundations were laid for the house of the LORD of Hosts, their promise that the temple 10 is to be rebuilt. Till that time there was no hiring either of man or of beast, no one could safely go about his business because of his enemies, and I set all men one against 11 another. But now I am not the same towards the survivors of this people as I was in former days, says the 12 LORD of Hosts. For they shall sow in safety; the vine shall yield its fruit and the soil its produce, the heavens shall give their dew; with all these things I will endow the 13 survivors of this people. You, house of Judah and house of Israel, have been the very symbol of a curse to all the nations; and now I will save you, and you shall become the symbol of a blessing. Courage! Do not be afraid.

14    For these are the words of the LORD of Hosts: Whereas I resolved to ruin you because your ancestors roused me 15 to anger, says the LORD of Hosts, and I did not relent, so in these days I have once more[a] resolved to do good to Jerusalem and to the house of Judah; do not be afraid. 16 This is what you shall do: speak the truth to each other, 17 administer true and sound justice in the city gate. Do not contrive any evil one against another, and do not love perjury, for all this I hate. This is the very word of the LORD.

\* 9. *These are the words of the LORD of Hosts:* verses 9–13 comprise a section longer than the brief oracles of which ch. 8 mainly consists and different in form and structure. It bears striking resemblances to 2 Chron. 15: 3–7. This suggests that here, as elsewhere, we have characteristic sermon material from the temple of about the time of the Chronicler. *you who*

[a] once more: *or* changed my mind and.

*in these days hear...:* an explicit reference to those who hear
and read in the later times of the editor the promises of the
prophets Haggai and Zechariah. The promises which they
attached to the rebuilding of the temple are to be fulfilled.
The judgements which they also, like the community of
Haggai's time, had known in hardship and suffering, are to be
fully reversed even although so far the promises appear to have
received only a partial fulfilment.

12–13. *I will endow the survivors of this people. You, house of
Judah and house of Israel...:* again the community is addressed
by the editor as 'the remnant'. For the reference to *Judah* and
*Israel* see the comment on 1: 19. Either the same hand has
added the reference to the *house of Israel* or the Judaean
'remnant' are seen as the true 'Israel', the true people of God.

14–15. *Whereas I resolved to ruin you...so in these days I have
once more resolved to do good to Jerusalem...:* another short
oracle on the theme of reversal of judgement, parallel to the
oracle attached to the first vision in 1: 12–16.

16–17. *This is what you shall do:* a brief summary of prophetic ethical teaching is added here, as in 7: 8–9. Its function
is to remind the community that the promise of God's
blessings places them under obligation to live lives worthy of
his purposes for them.  ✳

### JOY FOR JUDAH AND THE NATIONS

The word of the LORD of Hosts came to me: These are 18, 19
the words of the LORD of Hosts: The fasts of the fourth
month and of the fifth, the seventh, and the tenth, shall
become festivals of joy and gladness for the house of
Judah. Love truth and peace.

These are the words of the LORD of Hosts: Nations and 20
dwellers in great cities shall yet come; people of one city 21
shall come to those of another and say, 'Let us go and
entreat the favour of the LORD, and resort to the LORD of

22 Hosts; and I will come too.' So great nations and mighty
peoples shall resort to the LORD of Hosts in Jerusalem and
entreat his favour. These are the words of the LORD of
23 Hosts: In those days, when ten men from nations of
every language pluck up courage, they shall pluck the
robe of a Jew and say, 'We will go with you because we
have heard that God is with you.'

✼ 19. *The fasts... shall become festivals of joy and gladness for the
house of Judah:* this is Zechariah's answer to the question of the
embassy in 7: 1–3. Not only will the fast of the fifth month,
lamenting the burning of the temple, and that of the seventh
month, observing the murder of Gedaliah, become super-
fluous, but there will be no place for fasts of mourning at all
in the new age. For the community of Judah there will be
occasion only for the joyful celebration of the new acts of God.
The reason the answer has been separated from the question is
probably because the editor saw this as a fitting climax to the
oracles of hope in Zechariah. It is not clear what the fasts in
the fourth and tenth months commemorated. Possibly the
first looked back to the fateful breach in the wall of Jerusalem
(2 Kings 25: 3–7) and the second to the beginning of the siege
(2 Kings 25: 1). *Love truth and peace:* another addition, reminding the readers of the ethical conditions for entering the new
age and celebrating its joys.

20–2. *Nations and dwellers in great cities shall yet come...:* this
picture of a pilgrimage of the nations to Jerusalem draws on a
continuing strand of the Zion tradition (e.g. Isa. 2: 2–4 = Mic.
4: 1–3). If 2: 11 comes from Zechariah there is no reason why
this should not also. In both places the primacy of Jerusalem
and the role of its people as the medium of divine revelation
to the nations is stressed equally. Where Zechariah speaks
against the nations it is particularly against those who have
oppressed the people of God (e.g. 1: 15, 18–21; 2: 9). Its
placing here may have been suggested by the reference to

Judah alone in verse 19. Someone in the circle of tradition which transmitted the prophet's oracles felt that this presented too narrow and exclusive a picture to mark the climax of his teaching and so sought to bring out the full impact of Zechariah's own words about the 'nations'. The vision was a noble one and its transmission shows that the prophet found followers able to recognize the grandeur of his own thought among those who came after him.

23. *they shall pluck the robe of a Jew:* the primacy of the Jewish community in the self-revelation of God is maintained here. But someone has spelled out a very significant role of mediation for the Jews of the Diaspora. Not only will they themselves be able to come and share fully in the blessings of the new age, but, because of them, the Gentiles of the lands in which they live shall come also. It is perhaps the nearest to an active missionary concept of the mission of the Jews that occurs in the Old Testament, outside the book of Jonah. It is a suitable climax to the oracles of Zechariah concerning the significance of the temple for the coming time of salvation. It is a fitting tribute to him that those who passed on the tradition of his teaching could see such far-ranging consequences flowing from it. ✴

✴　　✴　　✴　　✴　　✴　　✴　　✴　　✴　　✴　　✴　　✴　　✴　　✴

## THE MESSAGE OF ZECHARIAH I–8

✴ Zechariah was a prophet of hope who preached good news concerning Yahweh's salvation of his people. This confidence was based on a lofty conception of God's power and will to save his people, whose hope depended not so much on their fidelity and response as on God's sheer grace. He sees an actual return to the land, a military and political deliverance and a restoration of well-being and prosperity. In addition he sees a renewal of the people by God's work of forgiveness and cleansing, as Ezekiel had done. There are signs, especially in

73

the first two visions, that his ministry began among the exiles in Babylon for whom he promised deliverance and return in the manner of Second Isaiah. This ministry was continued back in Palestine where earlier hopes were related to the completion of the temple. He is steeped in the Zion tradition that God has chosen the city as his own in which to dwell among his people. All the old hopes for temple and city, celebrated in their worship from long before, will be fulfilled. God will again dwell among them and guard Jerusalem, which will become the centre of enlightenment to the world and the object of the pilgrimage of the nations. He is influenced by earlier prophetic teaching, especially that of Ezekiel, whose predictions he sees as being fulfilled in the rebuilding of the temple by Zerubbabel. This reference to earlier prophets makes it likely that from the first there was an element in his preaching which called for right response from the people in the manner of the earlier prophets. He saw Zerubbabel and Joshua ruling jointly in the renewed community.

Like the oracles of Haggai, his message has been passed on by those who moulded it and applied it to the later situation of their own day. The outlook of the two groups which continued the tradition of the prophets, for convenience often referred to in the commentary as 'the editor', shared several points in common. Both refer to the restored community as 'the remnant'; both describe the willing response and obedience of the prophet's contemporaries, seeing it as a model to later generations; both see a link between the 'spirit of God' and prophecy. There is more stress on the future hope in the editorial material of Zech. 1–8, where it is emphasized that all the prophet's hopes will be fulfilled even if, up to that point, the signs had been disappointing. The call to prove worthy of this fulfilment and to hasten its coming by worthy ethical living is made even more explicit in this material. Here the nucleus of such teaching of the prophet is expanded in sermon-type material which we find also in the

Chronicler and which had probably become familiar from the preaching of the Levites in the second temple. A significant feature is the greater emphasis given to the priestly line. If Zechariah had attached messianic hopes to Zerubbabel, these have now disappeared. He is seen only as a temple builder with little political and no military significance. The messianic references are detached from him and cast into the future – a future which is assured meanwhile by the faithful, continuing ministry of the priestly line. It is through the priests that God's present and future plans for the community are fulfilled. Zechariah's hope for an involvement of other nations in the salvation of the Jews is preserved and underlined. Especial emphasis is placed on the Jews of the growing Diaspora who are not only assured of a share in the triumphant fulfilment of the prophet's hopes, but are assigned a significant role in their fulfilment.

These features suggest a slightly later date for the present form of Zech. 1–8 than for that of the book of Haggai. ✳

✳   ✳   ✳   ✳   ✳   ✳   ✳   ✳   ✳   ✳   ✳   ✳   ✳

# ZECHARIAH 9-14

✶  ✶  ✶  ✶  ✶  ✶  ✶  ✶  ✶  ✶  ✶  ✶  ✶

## WORDS OF HOPE

Hope for the future is one of the chief characteristics of Zech. 9–14. The process of relating Zechariah's promises about the temple to a still future hope was begun by the editor of chs. 1–8, as we have seen. It is carried farther in chs. 9–14. All mention of the building of the temple lies in the past and we no longer encounter any references to Darius I. There is now nothing corresponding to the visions of Zechariah and only in 11: 4–17 does the prophet speak in the first person. Such features of these chapters have led to the almost unanimous opinion of scholars that they are to be assigned to a different author.

Two notes are to be heard most clearly in them: one is concern for God's action in the future in judgement and salvation; the other is the note of controversy.

Hopes for the future are expressed in 9: 1–17 and 10: 3*b* – 11: 3, a collection of mainly poetical 'eschatological' oracles of varied structure and sometimes apparently inconsistent contents. 'Eschatological' here means 'concern with the last things', that is, with 'God's future action'. That action is viewed in terms similar to those of the earlier prophets who saw God working out his purpose in terms of this world's history, even if it were to result in the transformation of this world. In 12: 1 – 13: 6 and again in 14: 1–21 the theme of future hope is again dealt with, but here more in terms of 'apocalyptic'. In apocalyptic God's future action is seen as intervention from outside this world's history, renewing it completely in one decisive final catastrophe, since history is seen in more and more pessimistic terms. These differences only mark tendencies in these chapters: they are not 'apoca-lyptic' in the full sense. (For a discussion of apocalyptic see *The Making Of The Old Testament* in this series, pp. 51–3.)

The note of controversy sounds in 10: 1–3*a*, with its de-nunciations of the 'shepherds'; in 11: 4–17, in which a somewhat obscure act of prophetic symbolism is described whereby the prophet acts as a 'shepherd' to the flock, cul-minating in an oracle of judgement against the 'worthless shepherd' (verse 17); and in 13: 7–9, another oracle of judge-ment against 'my shepherd' (verse 7).

These chapters clearly had great influence. They are quoted more often in the passion narratives of the gospels than any other Old Testament prophetic collection, and greatly in-fluenced the writer of Revelation. The confidence in the final victory of God expressed in these chapters evidently proved inspirational through many succeeding times of crisis. The conviction that God himself would care for his people when their own 'shepherds' failed them kept faith alive in times of dispute and controversy, when the faithful felt themselves to be persecuted by the official leadership of the community. Some fine notes are heard in these chapters: the 'universalism' of 9: 6–7 and 14: 16–18; the care of God for his people (9: 8); the new values of the kingdom embodied in its representative (9: 9–10); the concept of God's spiritual renewal of his people (12: 10; 13: 1–2; 14: 20–1), and the vision of the ultimate universal reign of God (14: 9). It is true that other, less attrac-tive sentiments are also to be found (9: 13, 15; 12: 9; 14: 3) but such inconsistencies appear in most major prophetic col-lections in the Old Testament.

## WHEN WERE THESE CHAPTERS WRITTEN?

These chapters present a formidable number of problems. If they are not from Zechariah in the time of Darius I, who was their author and when were they written? Are they all the work of one author, or is there little or no unity in them? The widely differing answers of scholars to these questions show how difficult they are to answer. On the basis of supposed historical allusions within them they have been dated at very different times, between the period before the exile (seventh century B.C.) down to the second century B.C., in the time of the Maccabaeans. Some of the oracles in chs. 9 and 10 particularly have been said by some to be as early as, or earlier than, the time of Zechariah. Some have argued that these chapters are not all the work of one author, but of two, the first responsible for chs. 9–11 and the other for the more 'apocalyptic' chs. 12–14. It is to be noted that each of these sections is introduced by a separate heading, *massa'*, a word which meant 'burden' but also appears to have become a technical term for an oracle. The prophet had the sense of being 'burdened' with a word from God. Others have said that even the idea of two sections and two authors does not express adequately the great variety of style, form and content in these chapters. They say that Zech. 9–14 is a miscellaneous collection of isolated units loosely grouped round the general theme of eschatological hope. At the other extreme it has been claimed that these chapters reveal a clear and carefully formed structure and that this shows the essential unity of their final presentation. Such schemes, however, ignoring as they do the wide differences, argue more for the ingenuity of the commentator than for anything else. It takes a great deal of intricate argument to make the structure clear to the impartial reader.

Before such a bewildering variety of scholarly opinions the reader may well despair. The very variety of opinion is its own warning that the evidence which could prove any one of them is lacking. However, two characteristics of a general nature need to be noted. The first is that, for all the differences between Zech. 1–8 and 9–14, there are certain similarities. Among the emphases the two parts have in common are:

(a) The centrality of Jerusalem and common sharing of the

Zion tradition (e.g. 9: 8, 9–10; 12: 1 – 13: 1; 14: 1–21; cp. 1: 12–16; 2: 1–13).

(b) The cleansing of the community as part of God's final act (e.g. 10: 9; 12: 10; 13: 1–2; 14: 20–1; cp. 3: 1–9; 5: 1–11).

(c) A universalism which sees a place for all nations in God's kingdom (e.g. 9: 7, 10; 14: 16–19; cp. 2: 11; 8: 20–3).

(d) An appeal to the authority of the earlier prophets (this feature of chs. 9–14 is discussed throughout the commentary; cp. 1: 2–6; 7: 12).

(e) A concern with the problem of leadership as one sign of the new age (9: 9–10; and see the attacks on the 'shepherds' as false leaders, e.g. 10: 2–3; cp. the emphasis on Joshua and Zerubbabel in chs. 1–8).

The differences which have been rightly shown to exist between chs. 1–8 and 9–14 suggest that chs. 9–14 are from different and later hands than Zechariah. The similarities, however, suggest that chs. 9–14 may come from the continuing tradition in which we have already seen that the oracles of Zechariah were handed on. If so, they stand farther downstream in the history of the group which maintained and developed the tradition. Perhaps chs. 9–14 themselves represent a continuing development of the tradition extending over a considerable period of time.

THE REINTERPRETATION OF EARLIER WRITINGS

The second general characteristic of these chapters is their dependence on earlier biblical material, especially, but not exclusively, on the major prophetic writings of the Old Testament. This is a feature which has long been noted by scholars although it is not easy to demonstrate quickly, for direct quotations are seldom used (13: 5 appears to be a partial exception; cp. Amos 7: 14). Nevertheless the allusions are often unmistakable, especially to the reader of Hebrew and, given the cumulative effect, suggest an outlook which sees the words of the earlier prophets as the authoritative word of

God for all times. To some extent the prophet of the living word is giving way to the exegete of the written word. This does not mean that these chapters lack original ideas; what is new is expressed very often in the expounding and updating of already familiar material. Recognition that the material in chs. 9–14 is of this nature has important consequences for their interpretation. In the first place it cuts away some of the ground on which the chapters as a whole, or sections within them, have been dated by some scholars. They have often claimed to date them by the historical allusions they have discovered within them. An example of this is the belief that 9: 1–8 reflects the campaign of Alexander the Great against Tyre. If, however, much of the language and terminology is being drawn from earlier prophecy and used symbolically, the 'historical allusions' disappear. It might be, for example, that 'Tyre' in 9: 3–4 does not so much signify the historical city as a symbol of those qualities of pride and defiance for which Ezekiel attacked it (Ezek. 28: 2–10).

This may appear to put us back in our knowledge of these chapters but it has its own value for dating them. It suggests a time for their final form (whatever the date of origin of some sections within them) when it was believed that the authentic voice of prophecy belonged to the past. It suggests also that a time had been reached when at least some of the written collections of prophecies had been brought together, circulated and achieved some measure of authority. It is impossible to be precise about the time when this stage was reached, but it points at the earliest to the later Persian period (fifth to fourth centuries B.C.) and very possibly to the early Greek period (fourth to third centuries B.C.).

There is another important consequence of the literary dependence of these chapters, for it is found in all sections of chs. 9–14. It marks the eschatological oracles of chs. 9 and 10, the more 'apocalyptic' chs. 12–14 and appears also in the controversial passages of 10: 1–3*a*; 11: 4–17 and 13: 7–9. Again this suggests that, whatever the date of origin of some of the component parts of these chapters, and whatever inner inconsistencies are to be found in them, they must have been edited, used and presented by those who shared a similar outlook.

If these are justifiable inferences from the general nature of these chapters, the following tentative explanation of their origin and structure may be offered. They could mark the crystallization of the hopes and view-point of a group which was a continuation of that which had preserved and interpreted the oracles of Zechariah. They had retained his eschatological hopes even although they had modified them, and chs. 9–10 represent a series of eschatological oracles, perhaps of varied origin, which they collected, edited and issued to express their hopes. These oracles could well have served as a kind of eschatological 'hymn-book' for the community. As time went by, however, this group became more and more disappointed with the official leadership. History shows it was often corrupt, self-seeking, compromised and compromising. Compared with the hopes which Zechariah had attached to Zerubbabel and Joshua, and which his successors had attached more and more to the priesthood, they became disillusioned with the priests of their own time. This led to increasingly bitter attacks on the so-called 'shepherds' (10: 1–3*a*; 11: 4–17; 13: 7–9). Their failure to influence this leadership, indeed their rejection by it, led to a more and more radical expectation of God's future action. This was expressed in the more apocalyptic-type predictions of 12: 1 – 13: 6 and later, more drastically, in ch. 14.

It must be allowed, however, that a certain humility is required in both commentator and reader before these chapters. There is much in them which remains tantalizingly obscure and at times it is better to acknowledge that we do not know than to elevate clever guess-work to the plane of confident and dogmatic assertion. We must attempt to base conclusions on a study of the *nature* of the material. We must also listen for the message which spoke through these chapters and led to their being preserved, passed on and presented in their extant form. Their difficulties must not blind us to the fact that they proved an inspiration to the people of God through many successive times of crisis and change.

✳   ✳   ✳   ✳   ✳   ✳   ✳   ✳   ✳   ✳   ✳   ✳   ✳

# *Judah's triumph over her enemies*

## GOD'S UNIVERSAL RULE

**9** An oracle: the word of the LORD.

> He has come to the land of Hadrach
> and*ᵃ* established himself in Damascus;
>> for the capital city*ᵇ* of Aram*ᶜ* is the LORD's,
>> as are all the tribes of Israel.
>
> 2   *ᵈ*Sidon has closed her frontier against Hamath,
>> for she is very wary.
>
> 3   Tyre has built herself a rampart;
> she has heaped up silver like dust
>> and gold like mud in the streets.
>
> 4   But wait, the Lord will dispossess her
> and strike down the power of her ships,
>> and the city itself will be destroyed by fire.
>
> 5   Let Ashkelon see it and be afraid;
> Gaza shall writhe in terror,
> and Ekron's hope shall be extinguished;
> kings shall vanish from Gaza,
>> and Ashkelon shall be unpeopled;

[a] He has come…and: *prob. rdg.; Heb.* In the land of Hadrach he has…
[b] capital city: *or* chief part.     [c] *So one MS.; others* mankind.
[d] *Prob. rdg.; Heb. prefixes* Tyre and.

half-breeds shall settle in Ashdod,                        6
and I will uproot the pride of the Philistine.
I will dash the blood of sacrifices from his mouth    7
and his loathsome offerings from his teeth;
and his survivors shall belong[a] to our God
and become like a clan in Judah,
   and Ekron like a Jebusite.
And I will post a garrison for my house                8
   so that no one may pass in or out,
and no oppressor shall ever overrun them.
[This I have lived to see with my own eyes.]

* This passage emphasizes that God's rule extends over all
peoples and it thus provides a fitting introduction to the
oracles of chs. 9–10 which announce his final victory on behalf
of his people. It is a difficult passage because in several places
the Hebrew is obscure and offers various possible translations.
Its terse allusiveness has also given rise to many different interpretations. Verses 1–6a appear to be a series of threats of
judgement against various foreign nations in the messenger
style of third-person speech. They are similar to the oracles
of judgement against foreign nations which appear in all the
major prophetic collections of the Old Testament. In verses
6b–8, with the change of form to words of God in the first
person, there occurs a remarkable modification of the traditional threat against the nations. It is transformed into a
promise of the cleansing of the Philistines and their incor-
poration into the people of God.

   1. *An oracle: the word of the LORD:* the word for *oracle*
means 'burden' (see p. 78). It is not clear whether the phrase
*the word of the LORD* belongs to the heading, as the N.E.B.
has placed it, or whether it is the subject of the opening
sentence of the oracle. *He has come:* by substituting the subject

[a] his survivors shall belong: *or* he shall become kin.

*He* the N.E.B. assumes that something has dropped out of the text. It is not clear whether this is assumed to refer to 'God' or to some historical conqueror. It is just as likely that the subject is *the word of the LORD* which is spoken of as 'in' (or 'against') *the land of Hadrach*, and which 'has made Damascus its resting-place', the literal rendering of the phrase which the N.E.B. translates as *and established himself in Damascus*. In Zechariah's visions of the chariots (6: 8) the one which went 'to the land of the north', set God's spirit at 'rest' there, a different form of the word for 'resting-place' used in 9: 1. In that vision it marked the establishment of God's rule there and that may be the idea here. Whether it is the word of God, God himself or a conqueror through whom his purpose is accomplished, the emphasis is on God's rule being as effective in Syria as it is in Israel, as the phrase *for the capital city of Aram is the LORD's* shows. The Hebrew means literally, 'the eye of man is to the LORD'. The emendation of 'man' (Hebrew *'adam*) to 'Aram' (i.e. Syria; Hebrew *'aram*) is very slight, the Hebrew 'd' and 'r' being easily confused. 'Eye' may well be a metaphor for the capital city, Damascus, as the N.E.B. has taken it. *the land of Hadrach:* an area in the northern part of Syria known in Assyrian annals as *Hattrika*, near to Hamath, also in Syria. Why is Aram (Syria) mentioned here? Many commentators believe that the cities and towns mentioned in verses 1–8 depict the actual course of an invasion which the prophet sees as God's judgement against them. Among the campaigns it has been said to represent are those of earlier Assyrian kings, such as Tiglath Pileser III, Shalmaneser or Sargon; or Alexander the Great of Greece in the fourth century B.C. or the various campaigns of the Seleucid kings in the third and second centuries B.C. The passage offers insufficient details to identify it with confidence. But is the 'historical' explanation the right one? Syria, and the other places mentioned, could have been chosen as symbols. It could signify the 'north country' of Zechariah's last vision. Or again, since in these verses there are a number of allusions to the oracles of Amos, it could contain an echo of Amos 5: 27 where it is said that Israel will go into exile 'beyond Damascus' because of her idolatry. It was that very oracle which led the Qumran community to refer to the wilderness where they lived as 'dwelling in Damascus' (see *The Damascus Rule*, a manual of instructions for members of the Community, 6: 5, 6; 19: 7). They saw themselves as a faithful remnant living in an apostate age. The reference to Syria, therefore, may be symbolic. It may indicate that God is to root out the idolatry which has characterized not only foreign nations but also his own people and which has brought God's judgement on them in their history. His rule will be not just a geographical one but a total rule correcting men's tendency to apostasy and idolatry.

2–4. *Sidon has closed her frontier...*: the Hebrew has 'Tyre and Sidon'. It is unlikely that both are original since the adjective rendered by the N.E.B. as *wary* is singular. It is not easy to decide which was original. In any event the emphasis soon falls exclusively on Tyre. Tyre was famed for its wealth as a trading port. Ezekiel's attacks on Tyre for its wisdom, wealth and pride and his threat against her are closely echoed (e.g. Ezek. 28: 2–6; 26: 12). For Ezekiel, Tyre symbolized the pride by which man claims responsibility for his own achievements without dependence upon God. Again it is possible that the allusion to earlier prophetic material means that Tyre here is also viewed in a symbolic way as representing all human pride which will receive the judgement promised by the earlier prophets. *and the city itself will be destroyed by fire*: this echoes Amos' threats against a number of nations, including Tyre (Amos 1: 10) and thus paves the way for the references to the Philistine cities which follow.

5–6. In the oracles against Philistine cities there are also echoes of Amos 1: 6–8. The same four cities are mentioned (Gath being omitted in both) and similar punishments are threatened to different cities. The threat in Amos to 'wipe out those who live in Ashdod' is paralleled with the threat against 'the sceptred ruler of Ashkelon'. Here it is *Ashkelon* which is to be *unpeopled*, while *Ashdod* is threatened with a population of *half-breeds*. This word occurs only in Deut. 23: 2 where it refers to the descendants of mixed marriages who will be excluded from the cultic community of the temple. The threat to Ashkelon in Amos is echoed here in the warning concerning Gaza: *kings shall vanish from Gaza*. In Amos these attacks against foreign nations not only serve to establish God's rule over all nations, but lead up to the denunciation of Israel in similar, and even stronger terms (2: 6–16). Again then, use of earlier prophetic material may suggest that the Philistine cities also have a symbolic significance, being types of *pride* (verse 6*b*). As with Amos there may be a covert warning to the cultic community of a later time that they too will not be immune from such judgement.

7. In verses 6*b*–7 the transition to the words of God in the first person brings also modification from threat to promise of salvation. Philistia will be cleansed by God of all its *pride*, and *I will dash the blood of sacrifices from his mouth*: an allusion to the practice of eating animal flesh with the blood, a practice abhorrent to the Israelites and forbidden in the Law (Gen. 9: 4). *and his loathsome offerings from his teeth*: the eating of meats termed 'unclean' by the Law (Lev. 11: 2–23). Amos had said that 'the remnant of the Philistines shall perish' (Amos 1: 8), meaning that they would all be destroyed. This oracle transforms that with the promise that they shall become a remnant (N.E.B. *survivors*); see pp. 8, 17. Because of this they shall become a part of the cultic community as the Jebusite inhabitants of Jerusalem had done when, after David's capture of the city, they were integrated into the community of Judah. Ekron may be singled out because her hopes had been extinguished (verse 5) and so she typified those who had been purged of 'pride'. Thus the oracle of judgement is transformed into a remarkably universalistic hope of salvation.

8. *And I will post a garrison for my house*: the Hebrew is obscure and could also mean that God will himself act as a

guard at his *house*, a word which probably suggested the whole land of Caanan with the temple at its centre. In any case, God will see to its defence. The Targum (an Aramaic paraphrase) of this text links it with the similar promise in Zech. 2: 10, 'I will make my dwelling among you'. By adding 'in my holy house' and with the further addition from 2: 5, 'like a wall of fire', it suggests that this oracle was seen as sharing with Zech. 1–8, not only a universalistic outlook, but also a strongly Zion-centred tradition. [*This I have lived to see with my own eyes.*]: the bracketing of these words indicates that the translators believe it to be a later addition. It would be a comment by someone who sees the events being fulfilled in the events of his own lifetime. It could also be taken as a word of God himself, 'I have looked (i.e. on my people's affliction) with my eye.'

For all its difficulties this passage clearly makes a fitting opening to the eschatological oracles of these chapters. It emphasizes Yahweh's universal sway. It links with Zechariah's final vision, and so shows these promises to be the fulfilment of earlier prophetic hopes. It echoes the universalism and Zion-centred tradition of chs. 1–8 and the assurance of God's presence in his house as his people's defence. It assures the readers that all God's enemies will be overcome and the community cleansed to prepare it for the salvation to come. But, by its allusions to earlier prophecy, it may be reminding the community that the 'enemies' of God are not only foreign nations but the sins those nations typify. God can cleanse them from such sins, however. If there is hope for the Philistines, there is hope for all. ✻

### THE COMING OF THE FUTURE KING

Rejoice, rejoice, daughter of Zion,                    9
shout aloud, daughter of Jerusalem;
for see, your king is coming to you,
his cause won, his victory gained,

humble[a] and mounted on an ass,
    on a foal, the young of a she-ass.

10    He[b] shall banish chariots from Ephraim
    and war-horses from Jerusalem;
the warrior's bow shall be banished.
He shall speak peaceably to every nation,
    and his rule shall extend from sea to sea,
from the River to the ends of the earth.

✶ 9. *Rejoice, rejoice, daughter of Zion:* such a call to the community to joy is found in similar terms in Zech. 2: 10 and Zeph. 3: 14, which suggests it may have had its origin in the worship of the people (see p. 44). The change of form to that of a messenger proclamation suggests that this was a separate oracle but it has been fittingly placed after verses 1–8. After the announcement that God will defeat his enemies and rule from his 'house' (verse 8) the appointment of the agent through whom he rules in Jerusalem follows naturally. The qualities assigned to the king are significant for our interpretation of the eschatological hopes behind these oracles. *his cause won:* the Hebrew word behind this term, *tsaddiq*, can mean both 'victorious' and 'righteous'. The right relation of the king to God was very important (see Ps. 72: 1; 2 Sam. 23: 3–5) if he was to be a fitting representative of his people and truly mediate God's blessings to them. The idea is of 'victory' experienced because of this 'right' relationship. But the Servant of Second Isaiah can also say, 'one who will clear my name (literally, "pronounce me *tsaddiq*") is at my side' (Isa. 50: 8). *his victory gained:* this is a form of the verb 'to save', which can be either passive or reflexive. In its passive sense it occurs in Ps. 33: 16: 'A king is not saved by a great army.' The victory is not a human achievement, but God's. A related term is also used of the Servant of Second Isaiah who is sent by God 'to be my salvation to earth's farthest

[a] So Sept.; Heb. afflicted.    [b] So Sept.; Heb. I.

bounds' (Isa. 49: 6). *humble:* this follows the Septuagint, the Hebrew reading 'afflicted'. Both terms are used in the Psalms to indicate 'the poor', that is, the faithful who were suffering and needed help, often because of the persecution of enemies, and who recognized that God was their only source of help. The verb is also applied to the Servant: 'Yet we esteemed him stricken, smitten by God and afflicted' (Isa. 53: 4, Revised Standard Version). Some believe that there is an allusion here to the cultic celebration of the New Year Festival in Jerusalem before the exile, in which, it has been urged, the king was ritually humiliated. The term in Zech. 9: 9 has also led some to believe that this oracle came from the circle of the faithful in a time of persecution. *and mounted on an ass, on a foal...:* only one animal is meant, the two lines being an example of Hebrew poetic parallelism. The mount may not necessarily depict the humble mount of one who declines all the normal signs of royal honour. The ass was often ridden by kings in the ancient Near East (cp. Gen. 49: 10–11).

10. *He shall banish chariots from Ephraim and war-horses from Jerusalem:* the Hebrew has 'I will banish' which could be either the word of God or the word of the king. The promise should be seen against the background of the old prophetic denunciations of reliance upon horses and chariots and all human weapons of war (e.g. Isa. 30: 15–16). The king's dependence upon God will characterize the whole community of Ephraim and Jerusalem. This linking of Ephraim and Jerusalem suggests a hope that ultimately the former northern and southern kingdoms will be reunited. *He shall speak peaceably to every nation:* the final part of verse 10 closely echoes Ps. 72: 7–8:

> 'In his days righteousness shall flourish,
> prosperity abound until the moon is no more.
> May he hold sway from sea to sea,
> from the River to the ends of the earth.'

This gives strength to the views of those who have said that the roots of Zech. 9: 9–10 lie in the older worship of Jerusalem before the exile and especially correspond to some aspect of it connected with the king, perhaps to the king's annual re-enthronement. If so there has been a significant modification of the theme for Ps. 72 continues

> 'Ethopians shall crouch low before him;
> his enemies shall lick the dust.'          (verse 9)

In Zech. 9: 10 the king brings welfare (i.e. 'peace') to every nation by the word of his mouth, that is, by his just pronouncements. There is thus a pronounced universalistic tendency apparent in this oracle also. Because the king is the representative of the community, this oracle represents the kind of community hoped for by the circle from which these chapters come. Like Zechariah, it stresses that the Messiah, whose rule follows the destruction of the oppressor nations, will achieve God's purposes 'Neither by force of arms nor by brute strength' (4: 6). Traditional messianic features are modified by thought of a figure who bears some of the characteristics of the suffering Servant of Second Isaiah. Such lofty hopes go a long way to explaining the bitterness of the attacks in these chapters against the 'shepherds' who failed to evince the qualities this group looked for.  ✻

### GOD GIVES HIS PEOPLE VICTORY

11     And as for you, by your covenant with me sealed in
           blood
       I release your prisoners from the dungeon.*a*
12     (Come back to the stronghold, you prisoners who wait
           in hope.)
       Now is the day announced
       when I will grant you twofold*b* reparation.
13     For my bow is strung, O Judah;

[a] *Prob. rdg.; Heb. adds* no water in it.          [b] *Or* equal.

I have laid the arrow to it, O Ephraim;
I have roused your sons, O Zion,[a]
and made you into the sword of a warrior.
The LORD shall appear above them,
and his arrow shall flash like lightning;                    14
the Lord GOD shall blow a blast on the horn
and march with the storm-winds of the south.
The LORD of Hosts will be their shield;
they shall prevail,[b] they shall trample on the            15
    sling-stones;
they shall be roaring drunk as if with wine,
brimful as a bowl, drenched like the corners of the altar.
So on that day the LORD their God
will save them, his own people, like sheep,                 16
    setting them all about his land,
    like[c] jewels set to sparkle in a crown.

What wealth, what beauty, is theirs:
corn to strengthen young men,                               17
    and new wine for maidens!

✻ 11. *And as for you . . .* : the direct address in the second person feminine links this smoothly with the preceding oracle,
although the lack of further reference to the king suggests
that verses 11-13 form a separate oracle. It contains a promise,
similar to those of Second Isaiah, that the *prisoners* will return
to their land. *by your covenant with me sealed in blood:* a strange
phrase which has often been taken to refer to the Sinaitic
covenant which was sealed by the sprinkling of blood upon
the altar and the people (Exod. 24: 6-8). Others have taken it

[a] *Prob. rdg.; Heb. adds* against your sons, O Javan (*or* Greece).
[b] *Prob. rdg., cp. Targ.; Heb.* they shall devour.
[c] like: *prob. rdg.; Heb.* for.

as a reference to the sacrifices which were offered in Jerusalem. The Hebrew means literally, 'by the blood of your covenant', but could also be rendered as 'by your blood of the covenant'. It might then be a reference to what they have suffered at the hands of their oppressors, and take up Second Isaiah's thought that the Servant was appointed as 'a covenant for the peoples' (Isa. 42: 6, following the N.E.B. footnote). Their suffering was part of God's purpose for the nations. *I release your prisoners from the dungeon:* the Hebrew has 'from the Pit in which there is no water'. The last words appear to be a gloss overloading the line but suggest that someone had in mind the narratives of the release of Joseph from the pit (Gen. 37: 24) and Jeremiah (Jer. 38: 6) as both typifying God's deliverance of his people. The term 'Pit' is sometimes used for Sheol and so becomes a symbol of any kind of distress (e.g. Pss. 40: 2; 88: 6). Just what the distress is, is not clear. Second Isaiah used the term 'prisoners' to depict the exiles in Babylon (Isa. 42: 7) but when that same passage is taken up in Isa. 61: 1 it appears to be taken in a more metaphorical sense of the straitened circumstances of the returned exiles. The same more metaphorical sense could well be intended here.

12. (*Come back to the stronghold, you prisoners who wait in hope.*): round brackets in the N.E.B. indicate the view of the translators that the line is a later addition. Unlike lines in square brackets, however, this is held to be less certain and perhaps represents an addition by the author himself (cp. 9: 8). The word for *stronghold* occurs only here, but a form of the word is used in Isa. 22: 10 to describe the fortifying of the walls of Jerusalem (translated 'to make...inaccessible' in the N.E.B.). This may suggest that Jerusalem is in mind here, now garrisoned by God (cp. verse 8), and that this also echoes the Zion tradition. It is an invitation to those who are looking in hope for the final age to experience its fulfilment (cp. Zech. 2: 6–7). *I will grant you twofold reparation:* reminiscent of the promise to Israel in Isa. 40: 2 because 'she has received at the LORD's hand double measure for all her sins'. This is another

note of Second Isaiah which is taken up again in the later chapters:

> 'And so, because shame in double measure
>    and jeers and insults have been my people's lot,
> they shall receive in their own land a double measure
>    of wealth'  (Isa. 61: 7)

13. *For my bow is strung, O Judah . . . :* the picture of God's judgement in terms of loosing an arrow from a bent bow is a familiar one in the Old Testament (e.g. Ps. 7: 12–13; Lam. 2: 4). The N.E.B. takes the words *Judah* and *Ephraim* as vocatives, but the words can mean that God has made them his bow and arrow, and the last line of the verse supports this. It is possible that it has been understood in the light of the Servant of Second Isaiah, of whom it is said

> 'He made my tongue his sharp sword . . .
> he made me a polished arrow
>    and hid me out of sight in his quiver.'
>        (Isa. 49: 2)

If this is so, then the Servant's call to be a means of revelation to the nations is extended here to the whole people of God. The oracle would then be less hostile towards the nations than it appears. The linking of *Judah* and *Ephraim* may suggest a different origin for this oracle than 9: 9–10. *I have roused your sons, O Zion . . . :* the Hebrew adds 'against your sons, O Javan' (i.e. Greece). This is usually taken as a gloss (see the N.E.B. footnote) by someone who wished to relate the oracle to events in the Greek period. It certainly expresses the view of someone who took this oracle in a sense hostile to the nations. There might be a play on words, however. The consonants of the Hebrew word for 'Javan', pointed differently, could mean 'mire'. It might be intended as a disparaging epithet against the Greeks or, possibly, against the priests and officials in Judaism who 'bought' their office by bribing their Greek overlords, and so were 'sons of Greece' or 'sons of mire' rather than 'sons of Yahweh'.

14–15. *The LORD shall appear above them...*: these two verses form a separate oracle, again neatly jointed into their present context by the use of the word *arrow*. It uses conventional imagery to describe God's theophany (his appearance to his people, as in Exod. 19: 16–20) – trumpet, storm and lightning – and draws on the ancient idea of God as warrior champion, leading his people to victory. The origin of such imagery was the holy war concept from the days of the Judges, from which it passed into the cult (e.g. Pss. 18: 7–15; 77: 16–20). Verse 15 is extremely difficult to translate since the text is corrupt. The N.E.B. translation is as near as one can hope to get and gives a softer note to some of the harsher features which have been found here. With Yahweh of Hosts (note the warrior-title) they will be immune from harm, treading underfoot the harmless missiles of their enemies. They will know the boisterous joy of victory (a thought expressed less extravagantly in 10: 7), the joy of those who see God triumph over his enemies. The idea of God appearing to deliver his oppressed people occurs again more strongly in 12: 1 – 13: 6 and ch. 14.

16–17. Another oracle which switches abruptly from the tumult of conflict to the idyllic conditions which will follow victory. *his own people, like sheep:* in Ezek. 34: 11–16 the contrast is made between God as the faithful shepherd taking over the care of the sheep himself and his faithless shepherds, a contrast also stressed strongly in Zech. 9–14. *like jewels set to sparkle in a crown:* this echoes a saying found in Isa. 62: 3, 'you will be a glorious crown in the LORD's hand'. The translation *sparkle* follows an emendation of a rare verb connected with the word for 'standard'. Unemended, it could be rendered, 'like stones in a crown you will be prominent in the land'. This is similar to Isa. 62: 10, 'raise a signal to the peoples'. This itself echoes Second Isaiah's promise that God would make the return of the exiles easy by hoisting a 'signal' to the people (Isa. 49: 22). Perhaps the thought here, therefore, is that the restored people will themselves serve as a standard by which others may find their way to seek God. Just as the 'crown' in Zech. 6: 14 was to be a memorial in the temple to assure men that God's purpose would be completed, so the people here are seen as testimonies to God's purposes. *corn . . . new wine:* traditional features of the prosperity of the land of promise (e.g. Gen. 27: 28) and so of the prosperity of the new age (Ps. 72: 16). The phrase *new wine* also serves as a link word to connect this oracle to the previous one.

This short series of oracles, perhaps of varied origin, nevertheless has been arranged to give a complementary picture of the final triumph of the people of God. They show much of the spirit of Second Isaiah, often echoing his words in the more generalized way in which they are taken up in the later chapters of the book of Isaiah.  ✶

### WARNING AGAINST FALSE WORSHIP

Ask of the LORD rain in the autumn,*a*                    **10**
ask him for rain in the spring,
the LORD who makes the storm-clouds,
and he will give you*b* showers of rain
and to every man grass in his field;
for the household gods*c* make mischievous promises; 2
diviners see false signs,
they tell lying dreams*d*
    and talk raving nonsense.
Men wander about like sheep
in distress for lack of a shepherd.

[*a*] rain in the autumn: *so Sept.; Heb. om.*          [*b*] *So Pesh.; Heb.* them.
[*c*] *Heb.* teraphim.
[*d*] they . . . dreams: *or* dreaming women make empty promises.

3       My anger is turned against the shepherds,
            and I will visit with punishment the leaders of the
            flock;[a]

✻ This passage introduces a new note into the oracles of hope
for the future, a note of pastoral entreaty to avoid false worship, and of bitter controversy against false 'shepherds'. So
well has it been jointed into its context that it is difficult to
say where the oracle begins and ends. The thought of rain in
verse 1 fits well with the idea of fertility in 9: 17, so much so
that some have thought the new oracle begins there and the
N.E.B. opens a new paragraph with 9: 17. Again, verse 3
might well begin a new oracle linked to verses 1–2 by the
catchwords of 'flock' and 'shepherds'. It is likely, however,
that the new oracle begins in verse 3*b* with the change of form
from first-person to third-person speech. This marks the
change from threat of judgement to promise of deliverance.
The two would then be linked by the catchwords 'flock' and
'visit'. The second word is used in two different senses in 3*a*
and 3*b*. Unfortunately such a division means breaking in the
middle what the N.E.B. has rendered as all one sentence.

1–2. *Ask of the LORD rain in the autumn:* the words *in the
autumn* occur in the Septuagint, not in the Hebrew. They are
very probably original because of the association of the gift
of rain with the New Year Festival that was held before the
exile in the autumn (the beginning of the agricultural year for
ploughing and sowing in Canaan). The same association is
alluded to again in 14: 16–19 (one of the many parallels between chs. 9–11 and 12–14 which suggest that they come
from similar background). Both here and there it may well
allude to 'eschatological' rain, that is, to the conditions which
will make possible the idyllic fertility of the land in the new
age described in 9: 16–17. Later this is linked with the kingship of God (14: 9). *household gods:* literally, 'teraphim',
which had long been the subject of attack before the exile as

[a] leaders of the flock: *lit.* bucks.

objects of idolatry (1 Sam. 15: 23 – see the N.E.B. footnote; 2 Kings 23: 24). *diviners:* these had also been attacked by the prophets as false teachers (e.g. Mic. 3: 7; Jer. 27: 9). Since it is unlikely that teraphim were in use after the exile some have argued that this must be an older oracle dating from before the exile. More probably, the terms are used to symbolize all objects of worship other than Yahweh. This is more likely in view of the similarity of this passage to Jer. 14: 1 – 15: 4. This is a composite passage headed 'concerning the drought' and includes these words:

'Can any of the false gods of the nations give rain?
Or do the heavens send showers of themselves?
Art thou not God, O LORD,
that we may hope in thee?
It is thou only who madest all these things.'
(14: 22, N.E.B. footnote)

The passage in Jeremiah is strongly Deuteronomic in tone. It contains attacks against the prophets who are 'prophesying lies in my name' and who offer 'false visions, worthless augury' (verse 14). Indeed the point of the whole passage has been seen as a denunciation of false prophecy. The prophet of Zech. 10: 1–3*a* may well be recalling this to apply it to what he sees as the false worship of his own day. Like Jeremiah, he attributes this to lack of proper spiritual direction (verse 3*a*).

3*a*. It is the *shepherds* and *leaders of the flock* (literally, 'male goats') whom God holds responsible. This is similar to many passages in Jeremiah and Ezekiel bitterly attacking the leaders of their day whom they also designate as 'shepherds' (e.g. Jer. 2: 8). Ezekiel even uses the very term 'male goat' found here (Ezek. 34: 17). For the earlier prophets the false leaders would have been primarily kings, but the shepherds are so often paralleled with priests, prophets and wise men, that a more general sense of 'those in positions of responsibility' is not excluded. Similarly, the circle from which this oracle came appears to have regarded the worship of the official

Judaism of their day as little better than idolatry for which the leaders (by this time the high priests and priestly circles in general) bore a special responsibility. ✻

### THE RESTORATION OF GOD'S PEOPLE

but the LORD of Hosts will visit his flock,
  the house of Judah,
and make them his royal war-horses.

4 They shall be corner-stone and tent-peg,
  they shall be the bow ready for battle,
  and from them shall come every commander.

5 Together they shall be like warriors
  who tramp the muddy ways in battle,
  and they will fight because the LORD is with them;
  they will put horsemen shamefully to rout.

6 And I will give strength to the house of Judah
  and grant victory to*a* the house of Joseph;
  I will restore them, for I have pitied them,
  and they shall be as though I had never cast them off;
for I am the LORD their God and I will answer them.

7 So Ephraim shall be like warriors,
  glad like men cheerful with wine,
  and their sons shall see and be glad;
  so let their hearts exult in the LORD.

8 I will whistle to call them in, for I have redeemed
      them;
  and they shall be as many as once they were.

9     If I disperse them*b* among the nations,

[*a*] grant victory to: *or* expand.
[*b*] *Or* scatter them like seed.

    in far-off lands they will remember me
    and will rear their sons and then return.
Then will I fetch them home from Egypt        10
    and gather them in from Assyria;
    I will lead them into Gilead and Lebanon
    until there is no more room for them.
Dire distress*a* shall come upon the Euphrates*b*    11
and shall beat down its turbulent waters;
all the depths of the Nile shall run dry.
The pride of Assyria shall be brought down,
and the sceptre of Egypt shall pass away;
    but Israel's strength shall be in the LORD,    12
    and they shall march proudly in his name.
    This is the very word of the LORD.

✳ This passage is composed of a number of oracles in which the words of God in the first person alternate with third-person speech of the prophet.

3*b*–5. *the LORD of Hosts will visit his flock:* the use of the same verb *visit* as in 3*a* underlines the differentiation of fate within the community. When God appears it will mean judgement for false leaders but salvation for the hitherto misled flock (cp. verse 2). Jeremiah and Ezekiel also promised that God would shepherd his flock personally after the failure of their own leaders (e.g. Jer. 23: 1–6; Ezek. 34: 11). Some suspicion attaches to the phrase *the house of Judah*. It overloads the line, so destroying the parallelism. It may have been early comment by someone who interpreted the pictures of verse 4 in a messianic sense and recalled Jer. 30: 21:

    'a ruler shall appear, one of themselves,
    a governor shall arise from their own number.'

The abrupt change of picture from the people as 'sheep' to
[*a*] Dire distress: *or* An enemy.     [*b*] *Lit.* the sea.

*and make them his royal war-horses* must be intended as a deliberate contrast. The title 'the chariots and the horsemen of Israel' could be given to a prophet (2 Kings 2: 12). This suggests that the thought here is that the whole community of the faithful will assume the qualities and the role of former leaders. The N.E.B. rendering of verse 4 catches this exactly. The pictures used were applied earlier to leaders of the community: *corner-stone* to the Davidic king (Ps. 118: 22) and to other leaders; *tent-peg* to Eliakim, the king's steward (Isa. 22: 23); *the bow ready for battle*, while not used of the king in the Old Testament, was a royal designation in the Near East. Some of the Egyptian kings bore the title, 'He Who Repels The Nine Bows' where the 'Bows' were kings hostile to Egypt. In verse 4, however, the whole thought is in harmony with 9: 13 and suggests that these terms are now being used to describe the community of the faithful as a whole. This inference is strengthened by the word *Together* which the N.E.B. places at the beginning of verse 5 but which may just as well be an ending to verse 4. Verse 5 says that God's leadership will make the whole community victorious. The oracle as a whole closely resembles 9: 11–13.

6–7. Another oracle, introduced by words of God in the first person, followed by the third-person words of the prophet. *house of Judah...house of Joseph:* whether the reference to Judah in verse 3*b* was secondary or not, it is clear that this oracle, like 9: 13, envisages the restoration of both former kingdoms. *I will restore them, for I have pitied them:* a promise of restoration which closely echoes similar promises in Jeremiah and Second Isaiah, e.g. 'I will restore their fortunes and have compassion upon them' (Jer. 33: 26). *I will answer them:* this implies a cry of lament to God and so suggests something of a 'turning' to God. It echoes Isa. 58: 9:

> 'Then, if you call, the LORD will answer;
> if you cry to him, he will say, "Here I am."'

A complete reversal of the threat in Zech. 7: 13 is envisaged:

'As they did not listen when I called, so I did not listen when they called, says the LORD of Hosts.' Verse 7 recalls 9: 15 and provides another picture of the joy of victory.

8–12. An oracle which announces God's plan to bring back his people, now scattered, to their home-land.

8. *I will whistle...:* an unusual word for God's action in summoning his people back from their dispersion. Instances have been cited of the ancient practice of attracting a swarm of bees by whistling, a thought apparently behind Isa. 7: 18 where God summons Assyria and Egypt for judgement against his people: 'On that day the LORD will whistle for the fly from the distant streams of Egypt and for the bee from Assyria.' Now the former judgement is to be reversed. God is to call his own people home. *I have redeemed them:* a verb often associated with the exodus from Egypt and so used by Second Isaiah (e.g. Isa. 51: 11; N.E.B. 'set free'). Second Isaiah was speaking of the return of the exiles from Babylon. This must be thinking of the Jews returning from the Diaspora, or, more metaphorically, from the 'exile' of their distress. Both see salvation in terms of a second exodus.

9. *If I disperse them:* this rests on a slight and widely accepted emendation of the Hebrew which reads, 'if I sowed them' (i.e. like seed). It is possible, however, that with the emphasis in verse 8 on the great numbers who will return, the dispersion here is seen as part of God's preparation of his people for the last act of salvation, a sowing before harvest. It would then attach a preparatory and educative significance to the present distress. *and will rear their sons:* this underlines the point. In exile new generations of the people of God are being prepared. *they will remember me:* the word is often used of repentance and turning to God, corresponding to the 'I will answer them' of verse 6. The return is seen as more than a merely geographical affair.

10. Egypt and Assyria may be mentioned as traditional enemies of the former northern and southern kingdoms, or because they are the two nations mentioned in Isa. 7: 18

(cp. comment on verse 8). Gilead was a fertile region to the east of the Jordan which Israel occupied at times of national strength and prosperity. They never occupied Lebanon, but with its rich resources of timber from its famous forests it was a much-coveted area. The thought is that the boundaries of the land will be wide enough, and the land itself wealthy enough, to support all the numerous returned exiles.

11. *Dire distress shall come upon the Euphrates:* the text of the first part of the verse is unclear. The N.E.B. takes it in a way which gives good parallelism to the second part. A slight emendation of the text could also give

'They shall pass through the sea of Egypt,
he shall smite the waves of the sea.'

This rendering would again suggest a view of the deliverance as a second exodus.

12. *and they shall march:* Hebrew 'walk', which is often emended, but unnecessarily. The whole verse recalls Isa. 40: 31:

'but those who look to the LORD will win new
strength...
they will march on and never grow faint.' *

THE DOWNFALL OF HUMAN MIGHT

11    Throw open your gates, O Lebanon,
         that fire may feed on your cedars.
2    Howl, every pine-tree; for the cedars have fallen,
         mighty trees are ravaged.
     Howl, every oak of Bashan;
         for the impenetrable forest is laid low.
3    Hark to the howling of the shepherds,
         for their rich pastures are ravaged.
     Hark to the roar of the young lions,
         for Jordan's dense thickets are ravaged.

* This oracle is in the form known as a 'taunt-song', a form
often used by the earlier prophets to predict God's judgement
on his enemies. That downfall is so certain that the prophet
rejoices in it as though it had already happened. It can be
another form of a salvation oracle for the people of God.
Examples of it may be seen in Amos 5: 2; Isa. 14: 4-21; Jer.
6: 1-5. It is fittingly placed here since it links with the promise
of the preceding oracle that Lebanon would be included
within the territory of the people of God (verse 10), and the
recurring use of the catch-word 'shepherds', although these
are meant in a literal sense here.

1. *that fire may feed on your cedars:* judgement is pictured
as a sweeping forest fire destroying the wealth of Lebanon's
timber, the pastures by which the shepherds gain their living,
and the lairs of the wild animals. Taken literally it would
detract from the advantage of Lebanon being included within
the territory of God's people, but it is probably intended more
symbolically. Elsewhere the cedars of Lebanon symbolize
human might and pride (e.g. Ps. 29: 5). Whatever its origin
this taunt-song has been placed at the end of the oracles of
chs. 9-10 to express the conviction that all their hopes will be
realized since all that opposes the will of God will be destroyed.

In 10: 3b – 11: 3, therefore, as in the oracles of ch. 9, traditional prophetic themes have been taken up and applied to
a new and later situation. The outlook behind them all, with
the exception of 10: 1-3a, is still basically optimistic. *

### THE REJECTION OF THE SHEPHERD

These were the words of the LORD my God: Fatten the 4
flock for slaughter. Those who buy will slaughter it and 5
incur no guilt; those who sell will say, 'Blessed be the
LORD, I am rich!' Its shepherds will have no pity for it.
For I will never again pity the inhabitants of the earth, 6
says the LORD. I will put every man in the power of his

neighbour and his king, and as each country is crushed I
will not rescue him from their hands.

7    So I fattened the flock for slaughter for the dealers. I
took two staves: one I called Favour and the other
8 Union, and so I fattened the flock. In one month I got rid
of the three shepherds, for I had lost patience with them
9 and they had come to abhor me. Then I said to the flock,
'I will not fatten you any more. Any that are to die, let
them die; any that stray, let them stray; and the rest can
10 devour one another.' I took my staff called Favour and
snapped it in two, annulling the covenant which the
11 Lord[a] had made with all nations. So it was annulled that
day, and the dealers who were watching me knew that all
12 this was the word of the Lord. I said to them, 'If it suits
you, give me my wages; otherwise keep them.' Then
they weighed out my wages, thirty pieces of silver. The
13 Lord said to me, 'Throw it into the treasury.'[b] I took the
thirty pieces of silver – that noble sum at which I was
valued and rejected by them! – and threw them into the
14 house of the Lord, into the treasury.[b] Then I snapped in
two my second staff called Union, annulling the brother-
hood between Judah and Israel.

15    Then the Lord said to me, Equip yourself again as a
16 shepherd, a worthless one; for I am about to install a
shepherd in the land who will neither miss any that are
lost nor search for these that have gone astray nor heal
the injured nor nurse the sickly, but will eat the flesh of
the fat beasts and throw away their broken bones.

[a] the Lord: *prob. rdg.; Heb.* I.
[b] *So Pesh.; Heb.* to the potter: *or, with Sept.*, into the (temple-)foundry.

Alas for the worthless shepherd who abandons the    17
        sheep!
A sword shall fall on his arm and on his right eye;
    his arm shall be shrivelled
    and his right eye blinded.


✻ This passage is distinguished from the oracles that have
preceded it in 9: 1 – 11: 3 (apart from 10: 1–3*a*) in several
respects. Unlike them, its tone is wholly pessimistic; where
they predicted salvation, this announces judgement on
shepherds and flock alike; here the prophet speaks in the first
person and, apart from verse 17, the passage is in prose. Like
10: 1–3*a* it sounds the note of controversy. Opinion has been
divided over whether actual acts of prophetic symbolism are
described, whether the passage is to be understood allegori-
cally or whether it is a merely written imitation of the older
prophetic symbolic acts.

4. *These were the words of the LORD my God:* a most unusual introductory formula to a prophetic oracle or narrative.
The use of the term *my God* occurs often in the Psalms and in
prayers, but elsewhere is used particularly where a speaker
wishes to distinguish himself from his hearers (e.g. Josh. 9: 23;
Joel 1: 13). Its use here appears to set the scene for the prophet's
controversy with his hearers which follows. *Fatten the flock for
slaughter:* the word rendered *Fatten* means 'pasture' or
'become shepherd to'. It may thus place this passage among
the narratives describing the call of the prophets (e.g. Isa. 6;
Jer. 1). *for slaughter:* an unusual Hebrew word which occurs
only here and in Jeremiah. In Jer. 12: 3 the prophet says,

    'Drag them away like sheep to the shambles;
        set them apart for the day of slaughter.'

This is a reference to the wicked within the community and
perhaps, as Jer. 11: 18–19, 21–3 may suggest, particularly to
those who rejected the prophet and his message. Whether the

prophet of Zech. 11 saw the people as unworthy of his ministry from the first, or whether they are so described because of the way they afterwards rejected his ministry, we cannot say. Isaiah was a prophet the story of whose call, at least in the form in which we now have it, suggested that the ministry would be ineffective for the people as a whole (Isa. 6: 9-13).

5. *Those who buy...those who sell:* before the exile the prophets had attacked the wealthy who gained their wealth by the exploitation of the poor, sometimes literally driving them into slavery (e.g. Amos 2: 6; Jer. 34: 8-22). Even as late as the time of Nehemiah after the exile such practices seem to have reappeared (Neh. 5: 1-13). Such people now even go into the temple to praise God for their prosperity (and so cannot be foreign rulers). Thus they receive the approval of the official priesthood, no doubt in return for generous upkeep of the temple and its personnel. That is why it can be said, *Its shepherds will have no pity for it.* The tenses of the verbs in these verses need not be translated by the future as in the N.E.B., but even if they are, they clearly refer to events within the prophet's ministry.

6. A number of commentators have regarded this verse as secondary since it appears to extend the threat to *the earth* and because it introduces a note of hostility to the people, and not to the leaders alone. However, the description of the flock in verse 4, and the people's response to his ministry recorded in verse 8*b* suggests that, as in 10: 2, they are seen as corrupted by their leaders. Again, in verse 10, there is the suggestion that judgement against Israel has consequences for other peoples as well.

7. *I took two staves:* the act of prophetic symbolism with the two staves strongly recalls Ezekiel's action with two staves described in Ezek. 37: 15-28, where a different Hebrew word is rendered in the N.E.B. as 'wooden tablet'. The word generally means 'an article of wood' however, and more probably two staves were meant as the Septuagint under-

stands it. See the commentary on *Ezekiel* in this Series, pp. 251–2, on this point. But this implies repudiation of the promises Ezekiel's action expressed. The names of the staves are significant. *Favour* is a word often used for the presence and grace of God, as in Ps. 90: 17: 'Let the favour of the LORD our God be upon us' (Revised Standard Version); and in Ps. 27: 4, where the Psalmist longs to be in the temple, 'to gaze upon the beauty (same Hebrew word) of the LORD'. This thought of the temple as the place where the favour of God is made available to his covenant people is also emphasized in the interpretation of Ezekiel's action, 'I will put my sanctuary for ever in their midst' (Ezek. 37: 26). *Favour* is thus the experience of God that his covenant people enjoy, mediated to them by his presence in the temple. *Union* suggests a joining by pledge, the idea behind the root of the Hebrew word. It thus symbolizes the unity of the people of God by virtue of their mutual pledge of obedience to the covenant. Ezekiel was to join his two staves to symbolize the reunion of the old northern and southern kingdoms.

8–9. Verse 8*a* is widely held to be an interpretative gloss relating the narrative of ch. 11 to events of the glossator's own times. There is no preparation for the statement *I got rid of three shepherds*, and no comment on its meaning. There have been many guesses about the identity of the three shepherds but the statement offers insufficient evidence to identify them. Verses 8*b*–9 describe the rejection of the prophet by the people and his abandonment of them to judgement.

10. Unlike Ezekiel, this prophet announces judgement by breaking his staves. Leaders and people have proved unworthy, so they forfeit their covenant status and right to experience God's favour. *annulling the covenant which the LORD had made with all nations:* in the Hebrew this is in the first person, 'which I had made...' The N.E.B. is surely right to see in this a word of God. So solemn an announcement of the breaking of the covenant could only be spoken by God

who had established it. This again links with the passage in Ezekiel concerning the two staves where, as we have it now, the re-establishment of the covenant is associated with the joining of the two kingdoms. In this respect also Ezekiel's hope is reversed here. *with all nations* may allude to the idea that in the call of Israel God's purpose was to reveal himself to all nations, an emphasis found in Second Isaiah and Zech. 1–8. It is also alluded to in the Ezekiel passage, in a section expanding the message of the two staves: 'The nations shall know that I the LORD am keeping Israel sacred to myself, because my sanctuary is in the midst of them for ever' (Ezek. 37: 28).

14. *Then I snapped in two my second staff:* this announces the breaking apart of the old southern and northern kingdoms for ever, following the ending of the covenant relationship with God. The reversal of Ezekiel's prophecy is complete at all points.

11–13. Several factors suggest that these verses have intruded between verses 10 and 14, which originally were joined. Verse 11*a* repeats 10*b*; verses 10*b* and 14 parallel each other in form exactly; and verse 14 follows on logically from verse 10; mention of the wages for the prophet is not prepared for and diverts from the main symbolism of the staves, and no explanation of it is given. Finally, to see verses 11–13 as a fragment of the record of another, distinct act of prophetic symbolism, makes the symbolism of the staves more direct and easier to interpret. We are not told for what service the wages are paid. Possibly, before his call, the prophet held some official post in the temple. The significance of his action is not explained either, but there may be a hint in the phrase rendered in the N.E.B. *and threw them into the house of the LORD, into the treasury:* the word 'treasury' rests on an emendation of the Hebrew, which reads 'potter'. But the same word can also refer to a 'smith' who fashions in metal as well as clay. It has been argued that there was in fact a foundry in the second temple. Did the prophet throw the pieces of silver to be smelted in the temple foundry? A possible clue is provided by the Septuagint which adds a rider to the statement telling the prophet to cast the pieces into the smelting furnace. It adds, 'to see if it is good'. Did the prophet then repudiate the temple and the official priesthood by throwing his wages into the smelting fire? Did he intend thereby to show that the whole apparatus of temple and priesthood was to be refined by God to show what was dross and what pure? We cannot be sure, but, if he did, he would again be drawing on an oracle of Ezekiel (Ezek. 22: 17-22): 'Because you have all become alloyed, I will gather you together into Jerusalem, as a mass of silver...is gathered into a crucible for the fire to be blown to full heat to melt them' (verses 19-20). Such an idea would also be close to that found in Zech. 13: 9.

15-17. A third act of prophetic symbolism is narrated, beginning with a command of God. It continues, however, not with a description of the action, but with a statement of its significance. It is followed by a poetic 'cry of woe' over the worthless shepherd.

15. *Equip yourself again as a shepherd, a worthless one:* it has been argued that this would be a difficult act to carry out literally. It is possible, however, that it involved the prophet in appearing in the dress and with the equipment of a priest, or one of the temple personnel.

16. *I am about to install a shepherd:* this may be a reference to a particular high priest who the prophet felt was particularly unworthy, or refer more generally to the priestly succession as a whole. His qualities are exactly those denounced in Ezek. 34: 1-10.

17. The fact that this verse is in poetic form has led some to suppose that it was originally distinct and placed here on the 'catch-word' principle of editorial arrangement. Yet such 'cries of woe' appear in earlier narratives of acts of prophetic symbolism, as in Ezek. 24: 1-14. There the account of the boiling pot is twice interrupted in verses 6 and 9 with just such exclamations. *A sword shall fall on his arm:* this echoes Ezekiel's

threat against the king of Egypt (Ezek. 30: 21), which means
that Pharaoh will no longer be able to wield a sword. If, in
addition, the right eye is blinded, the shepherd would be
completely incapacitated and unable to withstand the judgement with which he is threatened. Physical incapacity would
also render him unfit for sacred office.  ✶

### A FAITHFUL MINORITY WILL SURVIVE THE JUDGEMENT

**13** 7*ᵃ*      This is the very word of the LORD of Hosts:
O sword, awake against my shepherd
and against him who works with me.
Strike the shepherd, and the sheep will be scattered,
and I will turn my hand against the shepherd boys.
8       This also is the very word of the LORD:
It shall happen throughout the land
that two thirds of the people shall be struck down and
die,
while one third of them shall be left there.
9       Then I will pass this third through the fire
and I will refine them as silver is refined,
and assay them as gold is assayed.
Then they will invoke me by my name,
and I myself will answer them;
I will say,*ᵇ* 'They are my people',
and they shall say, 'The LORD is our God.'

✶ By placing 13: 7–9 immediately after ch. 11, the N.E.B.
has rightly recognized that the passage belongs with it in
spirit and outlook, and is especially close to 11: 15–17.
7. *O sword, awake against my shepherd:* opinion has been

[*a*] *13: 7–9 transposed to this point.*      [*b*] *So Sept.; Heb. have said.*

sharply divided concerning the identity of the 'shepherd'. Is he the prophet who assumed the office of 'shepherd' in 11: 4, 7? Is he the 'worthless shepherd' represented in 11: 15–17? Or is he a good shepherd not referred to elsewhere in these chapters? Is he even 'him whom they have pierced' of 12: 10, or is he seen in messianic terms (cp. Mark 14: 27)? It has been argued that a worthless shepherd would not be referred to as *my shepherd* and certainly not in the phrase which the N.E.B. renders as *him who works with me*. The one Hebrew word which this phrase translates is a rare one, used almost exclusively elsewhere in the legal sections of the Old Testament which regulate the way Israelites are to treat their fellows (e.g. Lev. 6: 2). It thus suggests that the shepherd is a 'fellow' of God himself. Nevertheless, the terms used here, the reference to the sword of God falling, the word for 'striking', the references to the scattering of the sheep and the phrase *I will turn my hand against* are all used in the prophetic literature exclusively in a hostile sense and in a context of judgement. This suggests that the note of judgement against the 'false shepherds' is being continued. The point made in 11: 4–5 that the flock shares in the judgement of its leaders is thus maintained. The terms describing the shepherd apparently in a favourable sense must therefore be ironic. This is what they were meant to be by their calling.

8–9. These verses deal with an important issue to arise from the general threat to the community. Not all will be destroyed. One third will be preserved and tested and will emerge refined to a renewed covenant relationship with God. The symbolic act of Ezek. 5: 1–12 is recalled. Here he was directed to cut off his hair with a sword and divide it into three parts, all of which would be destroyed by various means. Originally the symbolism depicted the total destruction of the population in the fall of Jerusalem. Yet in Ezek. 5: 3–4 there is a secondary expansion of the original act to suggest that a 'remnant' would be preserved through all this. This is the thought which is developed in these verses. *I myself will answer them:* this recalls the promise of 10: 6. *I will say, 'They are my people':* that is, the old covenant relationship, annulled in 11: 10, will be renewed for the refined remnant (cp. Hos. 2: 23).

We have to decide how 11: 4-17 and 13: 7-9 are related to the oracles of chs. 9-10. The complete change of mood and tone has led many to deny unity to these chapters (see pp. 77-8). It is, however, a plausible suggestion that the prophet responsible for 11: 4-17 and 13: 7-9 found his ministry rejected and saw the official leadership of the Judaism of his day as corrupt and responsible for the blindness of the people. Warnings such as 10: 1-3a went unheeded. His rejection by them led to his rejection of them and of the whole of official Judaism expressed by the priesthood and temple worship. He now sees only judgement in store for the community and so announces the reversal of earlier prophecy, especially that of Ezekiel. Yet some did respond to his teaching and he sees them as the nucleus of a faithful 'remnant' who must undergo the judgement to come, but who would emerge refined from the ordeal (13: 9 and perhaps 11: 11-13) to inherit the old prophetic promises and to experience a renewed covenant relationship. Such a community must in fact have become a sect within Judaism just as later the Qumran Community were to become a sect rejecting temple and priesthood. They take to themselves now the promises expressed for all the nation in the oracles of chs. 9-10 (cp. 10: 6 and 13: 9). But in course of time they come to see that fulfilment of these promises will only be experienced after a radical process of judgement. So they come to the more 'apocalyptic' future view, expressed with growing severity in 12: 1 – 13: 6 and ch. 14. *

# Jerusalem a centre of worship for all men

✴ The repetition of the heading 'An oracle' at 12: 1 (cp. 9: 1) shows that chs. 12–14 were regarded as forming a new section by those who finally brought these chapters together. They differ from chs. 9–11 in depicting a time of distress and conflict before the final victory of God. They also differ in emphasizing the world-wide effects of the events of the end time. They are moving nearer to apocalyptic.

There is a certain general development of theme in 12: 1 – 13: 6 which gives the section a basic unity. The nations attack Jerusalem and are defeated by God (12: 1–9); this outward act of deliverance is accompanied by an inward act of cleansing and renewal of the people, leading to their penitence (12: 10 – 13: 1); the people then turn from their idolatry and reject the false prophets (13: 2–6). The often repeated formula 'On that day' and other differences of structure suggest that the section may have been composed from a number of originally separate oracles. The complicated picture of the relations between Judah and Jerusalem in 12: 2*b*, 4*b*, 6*b* and 7 may suggest additions to the text which sought to relate the passage to later events. The passage 13: 3–6 is a rather enigmatic and prosaic addition to 13: 2 and may well be secondary. ✴

### DEFEAT FOR THE NATIONS WHICH ATTACK JERUSALEM

AN ORACLE. This is the word of the LORD concerning **12** Israel, the very word of the LORD who stretched out the heavens and founded the earth, and who formed the spirit of man within him: I am making the steep **2** approaches[a] to Jerusalem slippery for all the nations pressing round her; and[b] Judah will be caught up in the siege of 3 Jerusalem. On that day, when all the nations of the earth will be gathered against her, I will make Jerusalem a rock too heavy for any people to remove, and all who try to 4 lift it shall injure themselves. On that day, says the LORD, I will strike every horse with panic and its rider with madness; I will keep watch over Judah, but I will strike 5 all the horses of the other nations with blindness. Then the clans of Judah shall say to themselves, 'The inhabitants of Jerusalem find their strength[c] in the LORD of Hosts their God.'

6 On that day I will make the clans of Judah like a brazier in woodland, like a torch blazing among sheaves of corn. They shall devour all the nations round them, right and left, while the people of Jerusalem remain safe 7 in their city. The LORD will first set free all the families[d] of Judah, so that the glory of David's line and of the inhabitants of Jerusalem may not surpass that of Judah.

8 On that day the LORD will shield the inhabitants of Jerusalem; on that day the very weakest of them shall be like David, and the line of David like God, like the angel of the LORD going before them.

9 On that day I will set about destroying all the nations that come against Jerusalem,

＊ 1. *This is the word of the LORD concerning Israel:* a strange heading since chs. 12–14 deal with Judah and Jerusalem. It

[a] approaches: *lit.* threshold.
[b] *So Vulg.; Heb. adds* against.
[c] The...strength: *prob. rdg.; Heb.* O inhabitants of Jerusalem, I am strong.     [d] *Or* tents.

may reflect a view which sees the 'remnant' emerging from all the upheavals of the last time as the true 'Israel'. *the LORD who stretched out the heavens:* a close echo of Isa. 42: 5. As with Second Isaiah it expresses the view that the final act of salvation is to be an act of re-creation, of a cosmic renewal.

2. *I am making the steep approaches to Jerusalem slippery:* an ingenious translation, resting on the fact that the Hebrew word usually translated 'cup' may also mean 'sill' or 'threshold', i.e. an approach to the entrance. Verses 2–9 envisage an attack by the nations against Jerusalem which will be frustrated by God's defeat of them. This is a very old concept which is expressed in a number of psalms (e.g. Ps. 48). Many scholars believe that such psalms form the liturgy of a great New Year enthronement festival in which the attack and the deliverance were enacted in ritual drama. It was taken up by some of the prophets as a picture of God's future deliverance of Jerusalem, and appears in various forms in such passages as Isa. 29: 1–8; Ezek. 36; 38–9; and Zech. 1–2. *and Judah will be caught up in the siege of Jerusalem:* the Hebrew is difficult and could also mean that Judah will take part in the siege against Jerusalem. If verses 4, 6 and 7 also suggest tension between the two, such an understanding of 2*b* would be possible, especially as this idea seems to lie behind 14: 14. Some manuscripts of the Septuagint have a variant reading at 11: 14 which speaks of the annulling of the covenant between Judah and Jerusalem, not Judah and Israel. This shows at least that the text could be so interpreted at times of later tension. However, it is doubtful if such a tension was intended in 12: 1–7 originally. In verse 5 Judah draws encouragement from the strength of Jerusalem. Verses 4 and 5 need suggest no more than the fact that the outlying districts of Judah would be the first to experience the effects of an invading army making for Jerusalem. Verse 7 seeks to emphasize that the victory would be God's alone and could not be taken as a 'right' of the community under the terms of a Davidic covenant or the special claims of Jerusalem on God's protection. Again, both Judah and Jerusalem are

said to be the objects of God's care and deliverance. It is probably best, therefore, to render verse 2*b* as the N.E.B. does. The phrase may still be a secondary, rather pedantic, addition to the text.

3. *I will make Jerusalem a rock . . . :* a phrase reminiscent of Isa. 28: 16:

> 'Look, I am laying a stone in Zion, a block of granite,
>      a precious corner-stone for a firm foundation'

*and all who try to lift it shall injure themselves:* literally, 'gash themselves', evidently a pagan rite of mourning, forbidden to priests in Lev. 21: 5.

4. *I will strike every horse with panic . . . :* a close echo of Deut. 28: 28, which is a threat of God's judgement against his people if they ever disobey the commandments of the law. It is now extended to all the nations who disobey him by attacking Jerusalem. This is an example of the way these chapters extend the judgement and salvation of the last times to a world-wide stage. *I will keep watch over Judah:* literally, 'I will open my eyes over Judah' and so, in contrast with the blindness of horses and riders, Judah will see where Jerusalem draws its strength (verse 5). It is reminiscent of the confusion of the Syrian army and the opening of the eyes of Elisha's servant at Dothan (2 Kings 6: 15-23): cp. 9: 8. Far from suggesting hostility between Judah and Jerusalem, it suggests a mutual encouragement of each other.

6-7. *like a torch blazing among sheaves of corn:* the same word for *torch* is used in the story of Samson setting torches on the tails of jackals among the cornfields of the Philistines (Judg. 15: 1-5). In the Old Testament fire is used as a symbol of judgement but also of the presence of God. Both thoughts are prominent here. The victory is really God's. He empowers the men of Judah. If they experience deliverance first it is because they are first in the path of the invading army. It also emphasizes that the victory is God's alone and not because of some guaranteed 'inviolability' of Jerusalem.

Verse 8 underlines such an understanding of verse 7. It is not anti-Davidic or anti-Jerusalem as such, although it does not suggest a strongly messianic view of the Davidic line. The line of David, like all other sections of the community, has cause for penitence and need of renewal. Since we cannot date this chapter it is hard to say what was understood by the reference to *David's line*. Was there still a governor who, like Zerubbabel, traced his ancestry back to the royal line? Was it believed that the ruler-priest had taken over the promises to David? Was it envisaged that at the last time the line of David would be renewed? We cannot say.

8. *the very weakest of them shall be like David:* a picture of the renewal of the whole community. All its members will know the relationship with God once thought to be the special prerogative of the 'sacral' king. To some extent this is a 'democratizing' of the messianic role (cp. Isa. 55: 3–5). *and the line of David like God:* a phrase which has caused much difficulty, so much so that many believe the phrase *like the angel of the LORD* is a later attempt to soften it. But the king had always been thought in a special way to be the mediator of God's blessings to his people. This envisages that the Davidic rulers of the end time, unlike so many of their predecessors in history, will be so close to God that they will act, speak and rule perfectly in accordance with his will. ✶

### THE RENEWAL AND CLEANSING OF THE
### PEOPLE OF GOD

but I will pour a spirit of pity and compassion into the 10 line of David and the inhabitants of Jerusalem. Then

They shall look on me, on him whom they have pierced,

and shall wail over him as over an only child, and shall grieve for him bitterly as for a first-born son.

On that day the mourning in Jerusalem shall be as 11

great as the mourning over Hadad-rimmon in the vale
12 of Megiddo. The land shall wail, each family by itself:
the family of David by itself and its women by themselves;
the family of Nathan by itself and its women by them-
13 selves; the family of Levi by itself and its women by
themselves; the family of Shimei by itself and its women
14 by themselves; all the remaining families by themselves
and their women by themselves.

**13** On that day a fountain shall be opened for the line of
David and for the inhabitants of Jerusalem, to remove all
sin and impurity.

* 10. *I will pour a spirit of pity and compassion:* outward
victory will be matched by an act of inner renewal, also
accomplished by God. The word translated *pity* also means
'grace' and 'favour', and is used both of men's showing
favour, i.e. compassion, to each other and of their finding
favour with God. In Zech. 4: 7 it is used to describe the completed temple ('men acclaim its beauty', the same Hebrew
word) and that completion was made possible 'by my spirit!
says the LORD'. Here he pours *a spirit of pity.* The word
translated *compassion* is also used of intercession for favour
and thus indicates a spiritual renewal. As a result they are
led to penitence just as in Ezek. 36: 31 penitence follows the
act of God's cleansing. *They shall look on me, on him whom
they have pierced:* a phrase which has proved one of the most
difficult to interpret in these chapters. Many have found it
difficult to understand how the people could have been said
to 'pierce' Yahweh, and so they have emended the text to
read 'they shall look to him whom they have pierced' (the
version found in John 19: 37). Others have taken it to mean
that they have pierced Yahweh by their treatment of his
representative. Some have rendered the verse, 'They shall
look to me. (As for) him whom they have pierced, they will
mourn for him. . .' Some have linked the 'pierced one' with

the good shepherd of ch. 11. Some have found a messianic reference here. Others have thought that there is an allusion to the Suffering Servant of Second Isaiah, or to a supposed feature of the earlier enthronement festival in which the king was ritually humiliated. Several have attempted to identify the 'pierced one' with some historical figure, e.g. Onias III, the high priest, while still others have taken the 'him' in a collective sense to represent the godly community which has been persecuted. Certainty must elude us, but some observations can be made:

(i) The more difficult text is probably the right one: 'They shall look to me...'; especially as it occurs in the context of penitence and turning to God.

(ii) The word for 'pierce' is used elsewhere in the Old Testament in a metaphorical sense (e.g. Lam. 4: 9, where the same word is rendered 'deprived' in the N.E.B., and Prov. 12: 18, where the sharpness of the wound of malicious gossip is compared to the 'sharpness' of the sword) and does not necessarily imply that the 'pierced one' was actually killed.

(iii) Their mourning over the treatment of the 'pierced one' is a work of God. It is the result of their repentance, not its cause, in the same way as repentance follows the cleansing work of God in Ezek. 36: 31. This does not suggest that the thought of a vicarious value in the death or sufferings of the 'pierced one' was prominent. It hardly suggests for him the role of a 'Suffering Servant', still less a messianic one. On the positive side it can be suggested cautiously that there might be a reference to the prophet and his circle, and that when the people return to God they will see that in rejecting him they have in fact been rejecting God and his word to them. They will look to God and mourn for the one they have treated wrongfully. The phrase could have been suggested by David's mourning over Absalom (2 Sam. 18: 33) or over his first-born by Bathsheba (2 Sam. 12: 15–23).

11. *as great as the mourning over Hadad-rimmon in the vale of Megiddo:* Hadad was the Syrian equivalent to the god Baal,

whose death and descent to the underworld were commemorated annually in a ritual of lamentation. It may seem
strange to liken the penitence and return of the people to
Yahweh to a pagan festival, but the implication may be that
they will see their former worship as having been little better
than idolatry.

12–14. The response of the families suggests the totality of
the mourning. Note that the royal house of David needs to
share in the penitence. *the family of Nathan:* usually taken to be
the descendants of David's son of that name (2 Sam. 5: 14). It
might be a reference to Nathan the prophet, however, so
indicating that the prophets join with the royal and priestly
families in mourning. Shimei was a descendant of Levi (Exod.
6: 17), so that royal and priestly families share in the penitence. But so do *all the remaining families*. The emphasis on
each family mourning *by themselves and their women by themselves* perhaps emphasizes the individuality of the response,
rather in the spirit of Jer. 31: 31–4 where it is said, 'No longer
need they teach one another to know the LORD; all of them,
high and low alike, shall know me, says the LORD' (verse 34).

13: 1. *On that day a fountain shall be opened. . . :* the perma-
nence of the spiritual renewal is guaranteed by the presence
of a continuing means of cleansing in Jerusalem. The reference
seems to be to a purified temple and cult. In Ps. 46: 4–5 and in
Isa. 8: 6 God's presence in Jerusalem is likened to a 'river'
and God himself can be described as 'the fountain of life'
(Ps. 36: 9). In Ezek. 36: 17 the same unusual word is used for
'uncleanness' (translated in the N.E.B. footnote as 'filth') as
in Zech. 13: 1, a term denoting the menstrual uncleanness of
a woman. ✳ (translated *impurity*)

THE REJECTION OF IDOLATRY

2 On that day, says the LORD of Hosts, I will erase the
names of the idols from the land, and they shall be remembered no longer; I will also remove the prophets

and the spirit of uncleanness from the land. Thereafter, if a man continues to prophesy, his parents, his own father 3 and mother, will say to him, 'You shall live no longer, for you have spoken falsely in the name of the LORD.' His own father and mother will pierce him through because he has prophesied. On that day every prophet 4 shall be ashamed of his vision when he prophesies, nor shall he wear a robe of coarse hair in order to deceive. He will say, 'I am no prophet, I am a tiller of the soil who 5 has been schooled in lust from boyhood.' 'What', some- 6 one will ask, 'are these scars on your chest?' And he will answer, 'I got them in the house of my lovers.'*a*

✷ 2. *I will erase the names of the idols from the land:* as in Ezek. 36, the promise of cleansing is linked specifically to the rejection of idolatry. It may suggest here that the worship of the temple then in practice was, in the view of the circle behind this oracle, little better than idolatry.

3–6. The rejection of the prophets seems a strange addition to the picture of the future in which these chapters draw so heavily on the prophetic tradition. It is usually taken to refer to 'false' prophets. It may be, however, that in their view of the future when God himself would again be present in his temple, there would no longer be any need for those who mediated his word. Again, it would be an application of the promise of the new covenant in Jer. 31: 31–4: 'No longer need they teach one another to know the LORD...' To appear as a prophet would be to cast doubt on the finality and totality of God's final act of salvation. Verses 3–6 seem like a rather laboured extension of this, possibly reflecting some later tension between rival factions or prophetic groups. *His own father and mother will pierce him through:* the same verb as in 12: 10. The inference must be that, whereas they wrongfully

[a] *Verses 7–9 transposed to follow 11: 17.*

pierced the true messenger of God, at that time the 'prophet' will be rightly 'pierced', for he will be false. *I am no prophet...:* seems to echo Amos' repudiation of prophetic status (Amos 7: 14). The obscure reference in verses 5 and 6 to what appears to be cultic prostitution suggests that this pretender is seen as no better than the old cultic prophets, some of whom were accused of compromising with the fertility rites of the Canaanites. The 'wounds' were those self-inflicted injuries caused in prophetic ecstasy (cp. 1 Kings 18: 28). Amos' words, which were understood to be his denial of the status of cultic prophet, are ironically used to suggest that this prophet shares the worst features attributed to them.

The section 12: 1 – 13: 6 lifts the final act of God's judgement and salvation more into the future and places it in a wider, cosmic setting. The deliverance hoped for in the earlier oracles of chs. 9–10 will now, it is seen, only take place after a dramatic assault on Jerusalem. The city and people will be delivered and final victory is assured, but only after a radical renewal of all sections of the community, not least the ruling and priestly classes who will come to see that their worship was little better than idolatry. They will see that in rejecting the prophet they have rejected God's true messenger. Such apostasy in the future would be prevented because in a purified temple the means of constant renewal would be available. This suggests a setting for the final form of this section at a later stage of this group's life and activity when their rejection had led to greater despair concerning the temple and official Judaism of their day.

Ch. 14 shows a certain unity of theme in its present form. The nations' attack on Jerusalem is again described, but unlike ch. 12 it is said that God himself brings them. The effect of the assault is much more serious for the city with capture and spoliation and the exiling of half the population. Only then does God intervene to deliver the remainder. Then God's universal kingship is established (verse 9) and a number of consequences of his reign are described. These include the transformation of nature (verses 6-7) and of the land of Canaan (verses 8, 10) with the elevation of Jerusalem (verses 10-11). The city, thus restored, becomes a centre of pilgrimage and worship for the nations (verses 16-19) and a place of holiness (verses 20-1). This general unity is the result of the arrangement of a number of apparently independent sections, marked by a change of person in verse 2 and the frequent occurrence of the introductory formula 'On that day'. Verses 12-15 and 18-19 appear to be secondary for reasons given below. In places the text is very difficult to interpret, probably because it has been considerably worked over, especially in the addition of a number of topographical details which remain obscure to us. ✶

### GOD'S DELIVERANCE OF JERUSALEM

A day is coming for the LORD to act, and the plunder **14** taken from you shall be shared out while you stand by. I will gather all the peoples to fight against Jerusalem; 2 the city shall be taken, the houses plundered and the women raped. Half the city shall go into exile, but the rest of the nation in the city shall not be wiped out. The 3 LORD will come out and fight against those peoples, as in the days of his prowess on the field of battle. On that 4 day his feet will stand on the Mount of Olives, which is opposite Jerusalem to the east, and the mountain shall be cleft in two by an immense valley running east and west; half the mountain shall move northwards and half southwards. The valley between the hills[a] shall be blocked, for 5 the new valley between them will reach as far as Asal. Blocked it shall be as it was blocked by the earthquake in the time of Uzziah king of Judah, and the LORD my God will appear with[b] all the holy ones.

[a] *Prob. rdg.; Heb.* my hills.      [b] *So Sept.; Heb.* with thee.

123

✳ 1. *A day is coming for the LORD to act:* a phrase which closely echoes Joel 1: 15 and 2: 1. Both this chapter and the book of Joel share a similar view of the cultic personnel of the temple and similar apocalyptic features in their view of the future. Both continue the prophetic theme, first introduced by Amos, of the 'day of Yahweh' as one of darkness. *the plunder taken from you shall be shared out:* a dramatic reversal of the promise made to Jerusalem in Zech. 2: 8–9, as though the present inhabitants of the city have shown themselves unworthy to inherit such promises.

2. *I will gather all the peoples to fight against Jerusalem:* a new and different emphasis from ch. 12. The nations are brought by God as his appointed instruments for judgement. There will be capture, plunder and exile for half the population. However, not all will be destroyed: *the rest...shall not be wiped out:* a 'remnant' will be spared although they will have to share the ordeal of the judgement. It is close to Isaiah's word at an earlier time of crisis for Jerusalem:

> 'If the LORD of Hosts had not left us a remnant,
>     we should soon have been like Sodom,
>         no better than Gomorrah.'          (Isa. 1: 9)

The verb 'left' is related to the noun rendered *rest* here.

3. *The LORD will come out and fight against those peoples:* an idea stemming from the old 'holy war' concept of God as the warrior who fights for his people, which had occurred in the earlier prophetic literature, e.g. Isa. 42: 13. It also appears in apocalyptic passages, such as Isa. 26: 20–1, which announces general woe for 'the inhabitants of the earth' and calls on the people of God to hide themselves while God's wrath is vented.

4. *On that day his feet will stand on the Mount of Olives:* a new oracle introduces the idea that the appearance of God in the divine theophany will take place on the Mount of Olives The phrase *which is opposite Jerusalem to the east* may be an addition to explain the reference to those of the Diaspora who do not know Jerusalem and its environs. However, it recalls

Ezekiel's vision of the glory of God departing from Jerusalem and halting 'on the mountain to the east of it' (Ezek. 11: 23), a departure due to the idolatry of the city (8: 15–18) and the sins of its leaders (11: 1–13). Later, when the glory of God returns to the city he comes 'from the east' (Ezek. 43: 2). If the Ezekiel passages have furnished the basis for the thought here, it may express the belief that the city of Jerusalem had become corrupt again, abandoned by God, and that the fulfilment of Ezekiel's prophecy had yet to come. The Mount of Olives is mentioned by name elsewhere in the Old Testament only in 2 Sam. 15: 30 when David went there after being driven from the city by Absalom's rebellion. Perhaps, therefore, associated with the name was the idea that Jerusalem's rightful ruler would come back to the city that way. Again, the 'height to the east of Jerusalem' was said to be the site for the temples to the gods Kemosh and Molech which Solomon built for his foreign wives (1 Kings 11: 7). Perhaps there is the overtone here that God's return in his city will bring an end to all apostasy. *and the mountain shall be cleft in two by an immense valley running east and west:* earthquakes were often seen as one of the signs of the divine theophany (e.g. Judg. 5: 4–5) and the idea here is that the valley thus formed will make a way for the triumphal entry of God into the city. It may echo the promise of Second Isaiah:

'Every valley shall be lifted up,
every mountain and hill brought down'
(Isa. 40: 4)

5. A very difficult verse which is probably an addition by someone who wanted to press the details of verse 4. The opening up of the east–west valley is said to result in, literally, 'the stopping up of the valley of my mountains', reading the pointing of the first word followed by the Septuagint and the N.E.B. Some have thought it implies the forming of a causeway across the valley of the brook Kidron, which runs roughly north and south to the east of Jerusalem. Thus it

would continue the thought of a divinely prepared way for the triumphal entry. Others have followed an emendation which would give, 'the stopping up of the valley of Hinnom'. This was a valley to the south and west of the city where refuse was burned and which also became the scene of cultic abuses (2 Kings 23: 10). This would certainly carry with it the idea of a purification of the city. *Asal*, taken by the N.E.B. as a proper name otherwise unknown, can also be emended to read, 'the valley shall reach...the side of it'. The text is too obscure for certainty. *Blocked it shall be as it was blocked by the earthquake in the time of Uzziah:* different pointing of the same Hebrew word can give either this rendering, or 'you shall flee as you fled before the earthquake...' Either is equally possible. The earthquake referred to is attested in Amos 1: 1. A tradition grew that Uzziah had been judged for some act of impiety (2 Kings 15: 1-5; 2 Chron. 26: 16-21). Josephus adds, 'a great earthquake shook the ground, and a rent was made in the temple and the bright rays of the sun shone through it, and fell upon the king's face, insomuch that leprosy seized upon him immediately' (*Antiquities of the Jews*, IX.10.4). This may be dependent on Zech. 14: 5, but it may suggest that a tradition had grown up that saw the earthquake as judgement for cultic apostasy in the temple by one who usurped the place of the rightful priesthood. If so, its mention here may suggest that this judgement will also be for the cultic apostasy of this later time. *and the LORD my God will appear:* the same title for God as in 11: 4 (see p. 105). *with all the holy ones:* the Hebrew reads, 'and all the holy ones with you'. This is often emended and taken to refer to the angelic hosts accompanying God. However, the 'with you', in the feminine singular, may refer back to Jerusalem and suggest that this was addressed to the community there. It is possible that the 'holy ones' refer to those who have remained faithful during the apostasy. They have been excluded from the city and temple but, when God appears, they will be restored to their rightful place in the community. *

### THE UNIVERSAL KINGSHIP OF YAHWEH

On that day there shall be neither heat nor cold*a* nor 6 frost. It shall be all one day, whose coming is known only 7 to the LORD, without distinction of day or night, and at evening-time there shall be light.

On that day living water shall issue from Jerusalem, 8 half flowing to the eastern sea and half to the western, in summer and winter alike. Then the LORD shall become 9 king over all the earth; on that day the LORD shall be one LORD and his name the one name. The whole land shall 10 be levelled, flat as the Arabah from Geba to Rimmon southwards; but Jerusalem shall stand high in her place, and shall be full of people from the Benjamin Gate [to the point where the former gate stood,] to the Corner Gate, and from the Tower of Hananel to the king's wine-vats. Men shall live in Jerusalem, and never again 11 shall a solemn ban be laid upon her; men shall live there in peace.

✻ A series of four oracles describing the transformation of the land, its seasons (verses 6–7), its fertility (verse 8), the universal kingship of God (verse 9) from which all these consequences flow, and the elevation of Jerusalem (verses 10–11).

6–7. These verses are difficult. It would be possible to interpret the Hebrew either as threat or promise. However, in their present context, they are probably meant to express hope, as the N.E.B. has taken them. They may echo the promise to Noah:

> 'While the earth lasts
> seedtime and harvest, cold and heat,

[a] cold: *so Sept.; Heb.* precious things.

127

summer and winter, day and night,
shall never cease.'                    (Gen. 8: 22)

This is more likely in that, in addition to the two pairs of nouns mentioned in verses 6 and 7, verse 8 includes the third pair, 'summer and winter'. If so, it is understood here as a promise that the realm of creation is to be restored. The effects of man's sin will be reversed, the promise to Noah fulfilled.

8. *On that day living water shall issue from Jerusalem:* an oracle which seems to recall the vision of Ezek. 47 of a stream of water issuing from the temple in Jerusalem and flowing to the eastern regions of the Arabah, bringing fertility to the land and even to the Dead Sea. It seems to be symbolic of the life-giving presence of God (see on 13: 1, p. 120). Here the waters flow east and west, perhaps an intensification of Ezekiel's promise. It is interesting that throughout this chapter the reference is to Jerusalem rather than to the temple, except in verses 20–1, where it is hinted that the temple will have no monopoly of holiness. It may suggest an attempt, not to exclude the temple from the work of God's restoration, but to show that the blessings to come will result from his presence and are not guaranteed by the mere presence of the temple in itself. Again, this may reflect an outlook which saw the temple of the present as a place from which the true worship of God had departed.

9. The great faith and hope of the old enthronement psalms, with their cry, 'The LORD is king' (e.g. Ps. 97: 1), will be fulfilled. In those psalms his kingship was associated with the defeat of his enemies, sometimes symbolized as 'the ocean' (Ps. 93: 3), sometimes as 'mountains' which are to be levelled (Ps. 97: 5), sometimes as 'nations' or 'princes' (Ps. 47: 8–9) or worshippers of other gods (Ps. 97: 7). It results in the establishment of God's rule in the natural order (Ps. 93: 1–2) and of his 'righteousness' throughout the world by his judgement (Ps. 98: 9). It results also in the elevation of Jerusalem as the centre of the world (Ps. 48: 1–2) and 'holi-

ness' in Zion (Ps. 93: 5). All these elements are present in Zech. 14. *on that day the LORD shall be one LORD and his name the one name:* there will be a return from all apostasy and idolatry to the pure worship of Yahweh according to the Law (Deut. 6: 4–5).

10–11. *The whole land shall be levelled...but Jerusalem shall stand high in her place:* this idea appears not only in Ps. 48 but in the earlier prophetic tradition (e.g. Isa. 2: 2–4 = Mic. 4: 1–3). Jerusalem, on high, shall draw all nations to herself as a place of religious instruction and enlightenment, an idea drawn out farther in verses 16–19. *Geba to Rimmon:* the northern and southern limits of Judah as in 2 Kings 23: 8 which speaks of Geba to Beersheba, with which Rimmon was closely associated (Josh. 15: 28–32). The concentration on Judah and the parochial details of Jerusalem suggest that this was originally a separate oracle from verse 9. *Benjamin Gate:* on the north side of the city. *the Tower of Hananel* and *the Corner Gate* are mentioned in Jer. 31: 38–9 where the rebuilding of the city is promised for the future. The location of *the king's wine-vats* is unknown. The emphasis appears to be on the size and security of Jerusalem and the mention of the particular locations may be to recall earlier prophetic promises concerning its future prosperity, purification and safety. ✳

### FURTHER REFLECTIONS ON THE BATTLE AGAINST THE NATIONS

The LORD will strike down all the nations who warred 12 against Jerusalem, and the plague shall be this: their flesh shall rot while they stand on their feet, their eyes shall rot in their sockets, and their tongues shall rot in their mouths.

On that day a great panic, sent by the LORD, shall fall 13 on them. At the very moment when a man would encourage his comrade his hand shall be raised to strike him

14 down. Judah too shall join in the fray in Jerusalem, and
the wealth of the surrounding nations will be swept away
15 – gold and silver and apparel in great abundance. And
slaughter shall be the fate of horse and mule, camel and
ass, the fate of every beast in those armies.

\* Verses 12–15 appear to be intrusive in their present position.
They interrupt the link between the elevation of Jerusalem in
verses 10–11 and the pilgrimage of the nations to the city in
verses 16–19. They revert to the war against the nations after
victory has already been described (verses 3–7). They add a
great deal of prosaic and largely irrelevant detail to the
account of the battle and appear to be dependent upon earlier
material. The section itself appears to be composite. Verses
12 and 15 belong together by their reference to the 'plague',
since the Hebrew word in verse 15 rendered 'slaughter' in
the N.E.B. is the same as that rendered 'plague' in verse 12.
Verse 13 adds a new note of divinely-wrought panic. Verse
14a depends on 12: 2 and 14b introduces a new note, the
bringing of tribute from the defeated nations. It looks like
a series of later attempts to explain in more detail elements
found in the apocalyptic section as a whole.

12. *and the plague shall be this:* the reference to plague here
and in verse 15 (see above) appears to be an attempt to
elaborate on 12: 4.

13. *a great panic, sent by the LORD, shall fall on them:* the
word for *panic* occurs also in the curses of Deut. 28; see
especially verse 28, where it is translated 'bewilderment' in
the N.E.B. It appears to be based on Zech. 12: 4 and to
elaborate it further.

14. *Judah too shall join in the fray in Jerusalem:* the N.E.B.
catches the possible ambiguity of the Hebrew here, but the
most natural sense of the words is that Judah actually joins in
the assault against Jerusalem. It is difficult to know whether
this rests on an interpretation of 12: 2b or reflects some

period of internal tension between the city and the country-side. *the wealth of the surrounding nations will be swept away:* the same Hebrew verb can mean either 'to gather' or 'to remove' so that it is difficult to know whether this is intended as the destruction of the nations' wealth or its 'gathering' as tribute by God's people. The thought of the bringing of the tribute of the nations is a familiar one, especially in such a passage as Isa. 60: 5–7. *

### THE PILGRIMAGE OF THE NATIONS TO JERUSALEM

All who survive of the nations which attacked Jeru- 16 salem shall come up year by year to worship the King, the LORD of Hosts, and to keep the pilgrim-feast of Tabernacles. If any of the families of the earth do not go 17 up to Jerusalem to worship the King, the LORD of Hosts, no rain shall fall upon them. If any family of Egypt does 18 not go up and enter the city, then the same disaster shall[a] overtake it as that which the LORD will inflict on any nation which does not go up to keep the feast. This shall 19 be the punishment of Egypt and of any nation which does not go up to keep the feast of Tabernacles.

On that day, not a bell on a war-horse but shall be 20 inscribed 'Holy to the LORD', and the pots in the house of the LORD shall be like the bowls before the altar. Every 21 pot in Jerusalem and Judah shall be holy to the LORD of Hosts, and all who sacrifice shall come and shall take some of them and boil the flesh in them. So when that time comes, no trader shall again be seen in the house of the LORD of Hosts.

* 16. *All who survive of the nations:* this could either be

[a] *So Sept.; Heb. adds* not.

editorial harmonization with verse 3, or an extension to the nations of the 'remnant' idea, linking with what was said of the Philistines in 9: 7. *to worship the King:* a link with the universal kingship of God, spoken of in verse 9. In Isa. 2: 2-4 (= Mic. 4: 1-3) the nations come to receive instruction. In Zech. 8: 22-3 they come 'to entreat his favour'. Here, they come as fellow worshippers alongside Jews. *to keep the pilgrim-feast of Tabernacles:* probably singled out for special mention because it was the great religious occasion of the year, the high point of Yahweh-worship. Further, it was clearly associated with the fertility of the land since it was an agricultural festival in which the gift of rain was seen as all-important. This is made clear in verses 17-19. It had already been alluded to in 10: 1-2 (see p. 96). The festival had a strongly eschatological flavour, so that for the nations to share in it meant that they too had a place in God's final act of salvation. This is behind the prosaic, rather laboured addition of verses 18-19. Even Israel's former oppressors, the Egyptians, may have a place, but only if they turn from their false gods to worship Yahweh. The festival was also closely associated with the kingship of Yahweh, a thought expressed in verse 9. This group has come to the profound insight that if God is equally king of all men, then all men may share equally in his blessings. It is called the feast of Tabernacles only in the later religious calendars (e.g. Deut. 16: 13). Earlier it was known as 'The Feast of Ingathering' (e.g. Exod. 23: 16), a kind of harvest festival, and it could be referred to as 'the pilgrim-feast' (e.g. 1 Kings 8: 2, 65) so important was it. Some scholars believe that the enthronement psalms (see on verse 9, pp. 128-9), celebrating the kingship of God, formed the liturgy of this occasion in Jerusalem before the exile. It is often referred to as the 'New Year Festival'.

20-1. Some commentators have found these verses an anti-climax after the universal sweep of what has preceded them. This is to miss their insight. *not a bell on a war-horse but shall be inscribed 'Holy to the LORD':* war-horses, often symbols of human might used in rebellion against God (see 9: 10), will now bear the same inscription as the high priest's diadem (Exod. 28: 36–8), and so all secular power will be under the dominion of God. *the pots in the house of the LORD shall be like the bowls before the altar:* even the ordinary temple vessels will be fit to use for the same purposes as the sacred bowls in which the blood and remains of the sacrificial victims were collected (Exod. 27: 3). Further, even pots in common use will be fit for 'sacral' purposes (verse 21). This is not only because so many worshippers are envisaged that all utensils will have to be pressed into service, but because the distinction between 'sacred' and 'secular' will be transformed. The whole of life, religious and secular, will reflect the covenant relationship with God which the temple worship celebrated. Since God is king, not only may all men know and worship him, but all of life can be transformed by him. *no trader shall again be seen in the house of the LORD of hosts:* the word for 'trader' is also that for 'Canaanite', perhaps seen as the symbol of apostasy and religious syncretism. There may also be an allusion to 11: 5, to those who 'bought and sold' the people, their unworthy shepherds. The temple and its worship will be utterly cleansed of all who have corrupted and perverted it.

There are obvious differences between ch. 14 and 12: 1 – 13: 6. The future ordeal for Jerusalem and its citizens is greater before God intervenes; there is no reference to human leadership, not even the muted hope attached to the Davidic line in 12: 7 – 13: 1; mention of the temple fades into the background; ch. 14 is more 'apocalyptic' in nature, its ties to events in history still looser than in 12: 1 – 13: 6. Yet both speak of a renewal and cleansing of the community; both speak of new springs of water; both show a similar dependence on earlier prophetic literature; both evince a critical, even hostile attitude to the cult and leadership of Jerusalem, although this is more marked in ch. 14, and both stress the centrality of a restored Jerusalem. It seems as though both do come from a similar group, but that the differences could be accounted for by seeing ch. 14 as coming from a later stage in their development. It represents greater disillusion with, and hostility towards, the official Judaism of their day. Reform is now despaired of. Temple and cult must be renewed by a drastic process of judgement and divine deliverance. Even so, the temple is hardly seen as occupying the exclusive place it once did, since all of life will have been 'sacralized'. We seem to see here the work of a group who in some ways anticipated the later Qumran Community. They too withdrew from the temple and condemned its priests and worship as apostate; they too re-interpreted earlier prophecy and applied it to themselves and the events of their own day; they too developed a strongly apocalyptic type of future hope.

Unable as we are to date chs. 9-14 of Zechariah with any degree of accuracy, they do suggest that the 'sect' type of community could develop within the life of Judaism after the exile and that we must look to such groups for keeping alight what they saw as the torch of the pure prophetic faith through times of persecution, apostasy and crisis. They were the forerunners not only of the Qumran Community but in some ways of the early Christian Church as well. It is perhaps not strange that these chapters are so often quoted and referred to in the New Testament. ✶

✶   ✶   ✶   ✶   ✶   ✶   ✶   ✶   ✶   ✶   ✶   ✶   ✶

# MALACHI

٭ ٭ ٭ ٭ ٭ ٭ ٭ ٭ ٭ ٭ ٭ ٭ ٭

## THE MESSENGER AND HIS MESSAGE

The book of Malachi opens a window on the little-known conditions of Judaism after the exile. It reflects the weaknesses which could assail it, with its bitter attacks on the laxity of the priests in the temple service (1: 6 – 2: 9) and the frequent indifference of the people to their obligation for the upkeep of the temple and its personnel under the law (3: 6–12). In it we hear the disheartened questions that must have been asked by a people who had so often been disillusioned by the apparent non-fulfilment of the promises of the prophets (2: 17; 3: 13–15). Nevertheless, it is certainly not the product of a mere legalist or ritualist who wants external observance of the law for its own sake. While it is harsh in its condemnation of the priests, it shows pastoral concern for the hard-pressed faithful, and meets their doubts by assuring them of the certain coming of God to fulfil all the hopes of the earlier prophets (3: 1–5; 3: 16 – 4: 3). It sees proper sacrifices and tithes as important because they indicate a real spirit of concern for God and a turning to him (3: 10). It re-emphasizes earlier views in the Old Testament of marriage as a covenant between two people before God (2: 14) and rejects divorce altogether on the humane grounds of the suffering of the wife who is rejected when she grows older (2: 13–16). It assures the faithful of God's love, even though at the same time it sounds the warning that the God who freely chooses can freely reject those who proved wicked (1: 2–5).

The writer reveals himself to be a man of deep faith and pastoral concern, but we have no direct information about him. Malachi may have been his name (proper names of this kind do occur in the Old Testament), but more probably it is a title meaning 'My messenger'. It is a term which occurs in 3: 1 of the one whose task is to prepare for the coming of God. Perhaps the author identified himself with this messenger, or was so identified by tradition. So his personality is hidden behind his role which was seen as the most important thing about him. At the same time, his very favourable assessment of Levi (2: 4–7) and his concern with matters of temple worship and priestly service do not preclude the possibility that he came from Levitical circles himself. Yet he stresses more the 'prophetic' aspects of the priest's office (2: 7).

The book consists of six main sections:

(i) God's love for Judah and rejection of Edom (1: 1–5).
(ii) Accusations against the priests (1: 6 – 2: 9).
(iii) A rejection of divorce and, as the book now stands, of marriages between mixed races (2: 10–16).
(iv) An answer to doubts about God's justice (2: 17 – 3: 5).
(v) A call for payment of tithes (3: 6–12).
(vi) Renewed assurances to those who doubt the value of serving God (3: 13 – 4: 3).
Two short additions conclude the book (4: 4; 4: 5–6).

Both style and contents show the book to be essentially a unity, although it has received a few additions in 2: 11–12; 3: 1*b*–4 and two separate ones in 4: 4 and 4: 5–6.

Malachi is characterized by a very distinct style in which each major section is marked by a series of questions and answers between the prophet and his hearers. This style of prophetic oracle is often referred to as a 'prophetic dispute'. It is found in Second Isaiah (e.g. Isa. 40: 12–17) and Micah (e.g. Mic. 2: 6–11). The question-and-answer style also occurs in Haggai's oracles (Hag. 1: 4–6, 7–11; 2: 3–5, 15–16). Indeed, there are a number of resemblances between Malachi and Haggai, not only in style, but in substance. Both lay great emphasis on the temple. For Haggai it is the building of the temple which lays a claim on the people's gifts and work; for

Malachi it is its upkeep and the proper observance of its worship. Both see the willingness of the people to respond as the pre-condition of God's blessing which is expressed in the fertility of the soil (Hag. 1: 10–11; 2: 15–19; cp. Mal. 3: 10–12). Both see concern for the temple as evidence of a return to God himself. Both assure their hearers of a coming deliverance by God. Some scholars have pointed to the similarities between the outlook of the editorial framework of the book of Haggai and that of the so-called 'Levitical sermons' recorded by the Chronicler. It is not impossible that Malachi came from just such a Levitical circle and so represents, to some extent, what might be called the 'Haggai tradition'. This would explain his emphasis on temple, priesthood and worship as valid expressions of God's presence among his people, while yet holding on to eschatological hopes.

### THE DATE OF THE BOOK

The question of the date of the book must still be regarded as an open one. It clearly dates from after the exile. The temple is standing and in 1: 8 the 'governor' is mentioned where before the exile it would have been the king. The term does not by itself tell us whether the book belongs to the Persian or the Greek period. The latest date is set by what appears to be a clear reference to the book in Ecclesiasticus (48: 10; 49: 10), so that it was known early in the second century B.C. Almost all commentators date Malachi between the time of Haggai and Zechariah and before the coming of Nehemiah to Jerusalem (445 B.C.), placing it nearer the time of Nehemiah. This may be right although the reasons advanced are all open to a critical reappraisal. It is true that some of Nehemiah's reforms during his second period of governorship, recorded in Neh. 13, correspond to abuses attacked by Malachi. But there are also differences. Nehemiah does not apply himself to the question of divorce while Malachi has nothing to say about Sabbath observance. It is said again that Malachi could not have appeared after the time of Ezra since the abuses he attacked would not then have been tolerated. This is to under-estimate both the capacity of abuses to recur in any com-munity, and the extent to which the Chronicler probably gives us a highly idealized picture of the role of Ezra. He probably attributed to him in one series of decisive actions reforms which more likely were long in the making and piecemeal in acceptance and application. It is difficult also to date the book by reference to Deuteronomy and the Priestly writing (see p. 9) and by trying to determine which of these two legal codes Malachi follows in his terminology for 'priests' and the practice concerning tithes for which he calls. Even if these were clear (see pp. 9–10) we do not know the date by which the Priestly Code was promulgated in its final form and accepted as authoritative. Even then we have to assume that it codified practices which had long been fol-lowed in some quarters. Nor does the reference to Edom help us, since we know little of the details of Edom's history after the exile, and it is not certain whether the reference is a literal one to the historical Edom, or whether Edom is being taken as a symbol of 'wickedness' (see p. 141).

We are forced back on much more general considerations of content and 'tone'. The fact that a clear distinction is being made within the community between the wicked and the faithful, for whom different fates are reserved in the time of final judgement, is an indication that we may be somewhere between Haggai and Zech. 1–8, and Zech. 9–14, where the process is taken farther. The eschatology here is not as developed as that of Zech. 9–14, with its picture of the assault of the nations and the sharing by all of the final ordeal from which the faithful community emerges refined. In Malachi the judgement simply reveals who is who (3: 18) and each is judged accordingly. Nor is there in Malachi anything ap-proaching a real universalism in the sense of other nations sharing in the salvation of faithful Jews, in spite of 1: 11 (see pp. 144–5). And Malachi is more interested in reform of the temple services and regulation of abuses here and now than anything in Zech. 9–14, where renewal of the temple cult and priesthood is entirely a matter for the future time of salvation. In this respect Malachi is nearer to Haggai and Zechariah than to Zech. 9–14.

We have then, for the present, to be content with very general and imprecise conclusions concerning date. The book comes from the time that elapsed between the ministries of Haggai and Zechariah and the final form of Zech. 9–14, possibly from the circle of tradition which handed on the oracles of Haggai and perhaps those of Zechariah.

✶    ✶    ✶    ✶    ✶    ✶    ✶    ✶    ✶    ✶    ✶    ✶

### MALACHI

An oracle. The word of the LORD to Israel through **1** Malachi.[a]

✶ 1. *An oracle:* Hebrew *massa'*. This heading also occurs at Zech. 9: 1 and 12: 1 (see p. 78). There it marks two distinctive sections of Zech. 9–14 and suggests that the two were seen as being related to each other in a special way. Its occurrence at Mal. 1: 1 may suggest that the group amongst which Zech. 9–14 circulated saw in the oracles of Malachi a welcome and congenial addition to their sacred writings. Features of Malachi – the denunciation of the priests, the criticism of temple worship, the division of the community into the wicked and the faithful and the assurance of a final deliverance of the faithful – all would have seemed closely related to the temper and outlook of much of Zech. 9–14. *through Malachi:* or, probably more correctly, 'my messenger'; cp. the N.E.B. footnote and see pp. 135–6. ✶

[a] Malachi: *or* my messenger.

# *Religious decline and hope of recovery*

## YAHWEH'S FREEDOM TO CHOOSE AND REJECT

2 I LOVE YOU, says the LORD. You ask, 'How hast thou shown love to us?' Is not Esau Jacob's brother? the
3 LORD answers. I love Jacob, but I hate Esau; I have turned his mountains into a waste and his ancestral home into a
4 lodging*a* in the wilderness. When Edom says, 'We are beaten down; let us rebuild our ruined homes', these are the words of the LORD of Hosts: If they rebuild, I will pull down. They shall be called a realm of wickedness, a
5 people whom the LORD has cursed for ever. You yourselves will see it with your own eyes; you yourselves will say, 'The LORD's greatness reaches beyond the realm of Israel.'

* 2–3. *Is not Esau Jacob's brother?*: for the question-and-answer style of Malachi in the form known as a 'prophetic dispute' see p. 136. Esau here stands for Edom (Gen. 36: 1). Edom was a neighbour of Judah, to the south and east of the Dead Sea. There was a long history of hostility between the two countries and their fluctuating fortunes were traced back into patriarchal times in the story of Jacob's supplanting of Esau (Gen. 27), which is also why Judah is referred to as Jacob here. In the story of the two brothers there is a recognition of the ethnic ties between the two peoples. This is recognized in Deuteronomy which speaks of Edom in friendly tones (23: 7–8) but in much literature of the exile and after a bitterly hostile note is heard, reflecting tensions difficult now to trace

[*a*] a lodging: *prob. rdg., cp. Sept.; Heb.* she-jackals.

in detail (e.g. Obadiah). *I love Jacob, but I hate Esau:* a harsh-sounding note of narrow nationalism which some feel contradicts a more sympathetic note towards other nations in 1: 11, and hence it is often assumed that 1: 11 is secondary. However, the 'universalism' of 1: 11 may not be as marked as some have found it (see pp. 144–5) and this verse may not be as 'exclusivist' as it sounds. It is probably an idiomatic way of expressing in Hebrew 'I have chosen Jacob rather than Esau', and corresponds to the use of the verb 'love' in an 'election' sense, as in Hos. 11: 1. No other nation but Edom is spoken of in this way, and it is possible that Edom is being used in a 'typical' sense, as symbolizing a 'realm of wickedness' (verse 4) on whom God's wrath (N.E.B. 'curse') will fall 'for ever'. If so, this oracle may not be as comfortable as it has often been understood to be. Why does a collection of oracles which so bitterly attack the sins and abuses of Judah begin with a reassuring reminder of their election? May not the main emphasis be on God's freedom to choose and reject? He does not reject arbitrarily. He rejects those who create a domain for wickedness. Then let Judah beware. As freely as he has chosen her in a covenant relationship, just as freely may he reject her. Paul quotes this verse in Rom. 9: 13 in a context which stresses the freedom of God to elect and reject whom he will (cp. 9: 18). This is also how it has been understood in Mal. 4: 6, an addition in which the people of Judah are threatened with the possibility that God will put their own land 'under a ban to destroy it'.

3. *I have turned his mountains into a waste:* it is not clear if this is a 'prophetic perfect' announcing a future calamity on Edom as though it had already happened, or whether it refers to some disaster in the past which we cannot now identify. *a lodging:* this follows the Septuagint and represents a slight emendation of the Hebrew which reads '(and I have given) his inheritance to the she-jackals of the desert'.

4. *If they rebuild, I will pull down:* such self-assurance explains why Edom can be called *a realm of wickedness.* Men

cannot hope to avert the course of God's judgement by their own efforts.

5. *The LORD's greatness reaches beyond the realm of Israel:* the same message as Zech. 9: 1–8, but perhaps with a note of warning as well as promise to the prophet's hearers. He is not bound to them in any narrow sense. ✳

### JUDGEMENT AGAINST THE PRIESTS

6 A son honours his father, and a slave goes in fear of[a] his master. If I am a father, where is the honour due to me? If I am a master, where is the fear due to me? So says the LORD of Hosts to you, you priests who despise my name. You ask, 'How have we despised thy name?' 7 Because you have offered defiled food on my altar. You ask, 'How have we defiled thee?' Because you have thought that the table of the LORD may be despised, that if you offer a blind victim, there is nothing wrong, and if you offer a victim lame or diseased, there is nothing 8 wrong. If you brought such a gift to the governor, would he receive you or show you favour? says the LORD 9 of Hosts. But now, if you placate God, he may show you mercy; if you do this, will he withhold his favour from 10 you? So the LORD of Hosts has spoken. Better far that one of you should close the great door altogether, so that the light might not fall thus all in vain upon my altar! I have no pleasure in you, says the LORD of Hosts; I will accept 11 no offering from you. From furthest east to furthest west my name is great among the nations. Everywhere fragrant sacrifice and pure gifts are offered in my name; for my name is great among the nations, says the LORD

[a] goes in fear of: *so one form of Sept.; Heb. om.*

of Hosts. But you profane it by thinking that the table 12
of the LORD may be defiled, and that you can offer on it
food[a] you yourselves despise. You sniff at it, says the 13
LORD of Hosts, and say, 'How irksome!' If you bring as
your offering victims that are mutilated, lame, or diseased, shall I accept them from you? says the LORD. A 14
curse on the cheat who pays his vows by sacrificing a
damaged victim to the LORD, though he has a sound ram
in his flock! I am the great king, says the LORD of Hosts,
and my name is held in awe among the nations.

✻ 6. *A son honours his father...:* a similar kind of opening to
the dispute found in Isa. 1: 2–3. Both start with a proverbial
saying which cannot be challenged, and then proceed to use
it to bring home their guilt to the hearers, in this case, the
priests.

7. *Because you have offered defiled food on my altar:* the priest's
task was to present the blood of a sacrificial animal and to
burn the fat or, in the case of a burnt-offering, the whole
animal, upon the altar. Any animal offered for sacrifice had
to be 'without blemish' (e.g. Lev. 1: 3) and no doubt it was
the responsibility of the priests to determine whether the
animal was acceptable. The Priestly Code explicitly says that
to eat unclean flesh of sacrifice, or to offer sacrifice while in a
state of ritual uncleanness would bring excommunication
from the people of God (Lev. 7: 19–21). By admitting im-
perfect animals for sacrifice the priests were offering that
which was unclean and laying themselves under judgement.
Such conduct was not just a breach of ceremonial regulations.
It betrayed a neglect of God which affected the whole community (verse 6). Haggai saw indifference towards God as the
true reason for their failure to build the temple. Malachi sees
the same cause behind their carelessness about worship.

8. *If you brought such a gift to the governor...:* governors are
[a] *Prob. rdg., cp. Targ.; Heb. adds* its produce.

143

mentioned from the time of the return from exile. Both Sheshbazzar (Ezra 5: 14) and Zerubbabel (Hag. 1: 1) are so described, and Nehemiah speaks of governors before him (Neh. 5: 15). The same reference shows that they were maintained by taxes levied on the people, and that is the point of the reference here. It is not clear what the exact extent of their authority was (see p. 14).

9. *if you do this, will he withhold his favour from you?*: the Hebrew is difficult and reads literally, 'this is from your hands, will he turn his face from you?' It may be a general call to repentance as the N.E.B. takes it, with the assurance of forgiveness if they entreat God's favour; it may be ironic, 'while you entreat his favour in this way, will you experience it?'; or it may be a call to repent 'because you have brought this upon yourselves'.

10. *Better far that one of you should close the great door altogether . . .*: a savage denunciation of the temple worship as it is conducted by the priests. The reference is probably to the door into the temple from the court of priests (2 Chron. 4: 9). Excommunication should be their judgement.

11. *From furthest east to furthest west my name is great among the nations*: the opening phrase is literally, 'from the rising of the sun to its setting . . .', a phrase which echoes Ps. 50: 1. That psalm contains a rejection of animal sacrifice because all the earth and its produce is God's. He wants the 'sacrifice of thanksgiving' (verse 14) and of right living. Such an idea may help to explain what is meant in these verses. *Everywhere fragrant sacrifice and pure gifts are offered in my name*: it is interesting that no sacrifice involving blood is mentioned, but incense and cereal offerings. The second of these can mean simply 'a gift', as the N.E.B. takes it. The reference may therefore be to the fact that when men anywhere acknowledge the mystery of creation and give thanks for it they are in fact acknowledging the greatness of the Creator's name (cp. verse 14*b*). Such worship, even if offered in ignorance of Yahweh's name, is more acceptable to him as offerings and gifts in their genuine-

ness than the blood sacrifices offered by the priests in the temple
in a spirit of indifference. The verse should not therefore be
rejected as secondary because its 'universalism' contradicts
1: 3. It is not picturing a universal conversion to Yahwism any
more than 1: 3 is suggesting an outright rejection of all other
nations. Neither should it be excluded because it interrupts the
connection between verses 6–10 and 12–14. The whole oracle
falls into two parts, verses 6–11 and verses 12–14, in each of
which similar statements of the charges against the priests
lead to a similar climax. The repetition is probably for
emphasis.

14. *I am the great king...and my name is held in awe among the
nations:* this verse drives home the lesson of verse 11. It is
not meant that all nations worship Yahweh by name. Because
he is king of all creation, however, when men worship the
Creator they are really honouring Yahweh with a sincerity
and zeal which shames the priests who claim to minister in
his name. ✻

### GOD'S COVENANT WITH LEVI

And now, you priests, this decree is for you: if you will **2** 1, 2
not listen to me and pay heed to the honouring of my
name, says the LORD of Hosts, then I will lay a curse upon
you. I will turn your blessings into a curse; yes, into a
curse, because you pay no heed. I will cut off[a] your arm,[b] 3
fling offal in your faces, the offal of your pilgrim-feasts,
and I will banish you from my presence.[c] Then you will 4
know that I have issued this decree against you: my
covenant with Levi falls to the ground, says the LORD of
Hosts. My covenant was with him: I bestowed life and 5

[a] cut off: *so Sept.; Heb.* rebuke.     [b] *Or* posterity.
[c] and...presence: *prob. rdg., cp. Sept.; Heb.* and he will take you away
unto him.

prosperity on him; I laid on him the duty of reverence,
6 he revered me and lived in awe of my name. The instruction he gave was true, and no word of injustice fell
from his lips; he walked in harmony with me and in
7 uprightness, and he turned many back from sin. For men
hang upon the words of the priest and seek knowledge
and instruction from him, because he is the messenger of
8 the Lord of Hosts. But you have turned away from that
course; you have made many stumble with your instruction; you have set at nought the covenant with the
9 Levites, says the Lord of Hosts. So I, in my turn, have
made you despicable and mean in the eyes of the people,
in so far as you disregard my ways and show partiality in
your instruction.

✶ 2. *I will lay a curse upon you:* Deut. 27–8 contains the curses
with which the Israelites were threatened if they broke the
terms of the covenant. In the dispute-style of Malachi a series
of 'curses' is uttered against those who have broken the
terms of the covenant. *I will turn your blessings into a curse:*
these could be either the blessings the priest pronounces
which will become valueless, or the blessings the priestly line
receives, perhaps a reference to gifts for their upkeep.

3. *I will cut off your arm:* this follows the Septuagint and
implies that the priests will no longer be able to raise their
right hand to pronounce the blessing. The Hebrew has, 'I will
rebuke your descendants'; cp. the N.E.B. footnote, 'posterity',
implying a judgement on the whole priestly line. *fling offal in
your faces:* unclean, the priests will be unable to perform their
sacrificial duties. *I will banish you from my presence:* the N.E.B.
rightly follows the Septuagint here. This shows that the
promise to Joshua recorded in Zech. 3: 7, which was conditional on the faithful conduct of the priest, is now to be
annulled.

4. *my covenant with Levi falls to the ground:* the N.E.B. rendering rests on an emendation. The Hebrew text reads, 'Then you will know that I issued this decree to you, that my covenant should be with Levi.' Such a covenant is not mentioned in the Old Testament although it is presupposed in Jer. 33: 21. In Num. 25: 11–13 a covenant with the Aaronite priesthood is recorded. If the N.E.B. emendation is followed, it suggests that the priests generally are being described as 'Levites' and that, because of their faithlessness, God is taking away the special responsibilities to which he appointed them. The Hebrew text as it stands, however, might suggest that the Levites are being distinguished from the priesthood as a whole. The priests are condemned, but the covenant God made with the Levites is confirmed.

5. *I bestowed life and prosperity on him:* in this and the following verses the qualities and duties assigned to Joshua in Zech. 3: 7 are recalled.

6. *The instruction he gave was true:* a reminder that the priest not only interceded with God on behalf of men but gave directions to men concerning the requirements of God.

7. *he is the messenger of the LORD of Hosts:* the teaching role of the priests is again emphasized in this verse. This is the only place in the Old Testament where the term *messenger* is used of the priest rather than the prophet.

8. *you have set at nought the covenant with the Levites:* by their conduct the priests have failed to honour their sacred calling. By breaking their obligations under the covenant they have forfeited the special status it conferred on them.

9. *I...have made you despicable and mean in the eyes of the people:* the result of their contempt for God is that they and their office have earned the contempt of the people.

The question remains whether any distinction is being made between 'priests' and 'Levites' in this passage. In Deuteronomy all priests are Levites and all Levites priests without distinction. In Ezekiel the priests are called 'sons of Zadok' and are distinguished from the Levites who are in the process of being demoted to the role of temple assistants (Ezek. 44: 10–14). In the Priestly Code the priests are called 'sons of Aaron' and the demotion of the Levites is complete (Num. 3: 5–10). A very favourable picture of the role of the Levites is drawn in verses 5–9 here, with special emphasis on their teaching role. This could mean that, if the Hebrew text (attested by all the Versions) is followed, Malachi represents a Levitical viewpoint and that it is the Zadokite/Aaronite priesthood which is being attacked. By contrast, God confirms his 'covenant with Levi' so disowning the secondary role to which they have been assigned since the return from exile. This is not certain, but it would strengthen the view that Malachi has some kinship with the tradition in which the oracles of Haggai and Zechariah were handed down. This also, as we have seen, shared certain Levitical characteristics. *

### A CALL FOR FAITHFULNESS IN MARRIAGE

10    Have we not all one father? Did not one God create us? Why do we violate the covenant of our forefathers by 11 being faithless to one another? Judah is faithless, and abominable things are done in Israel and in Jerusalem; Judah has violated the holiness of the LORD by loving and 12 marrying daughters of a foreign god. May the LORD banish any who do this from the dwellings of Jacob, nomads or settlers, even though they bring offerings to the LORD of Hosts.

13    Here is another thing that you do: you weep and moan, and you drown the altar of the LORD with tears, but he still refuses to look at the offering or receive an 14 acceptable gift from you. You ask why. It is because the LORD has borne witness against you on behalf of the wife of your youth. You have been unfaithful to her, though

she is your partner and your wife by solemn covenant.
Did not the one God make her, both flesh and spirit? 15
And what does the one God require but godly children?
Keep watch on your spirit, and do not be[a] unfaithful to
the wife of your youth. If a man divorces or puts away 16
his spouse, he overwhelms her with cruelty, says the
LORD of Hosts the God of Israel. Keep watch on your
spirit, and do not be unfaithful.

\* 10. *Have we not all one father?:* the parallelism suggests that
the reference is to God rather than to Abraham. This new
section is addressed not only to the priests but to the whole
community. *Why do we violate the covenant of our forefathers...?:* as the priests had broken their special covenant
by their faithlessness, the people as a whole had violated the
covenant by their faithlessness in their marriage relationships.
This shows an acute awareness that the terms of the covenant
bound them in loyalty to each other as well as to God.

11–12. These verses are secondary. This is shown by the
change from first to third person; by the break in thought
between the charge of mutual faithlessness in verse 10 and the
application of that charge in verses 13–16 which speaks of their
harsh treatment of their own Jewish wives. To this the charge
of intermarriage with foreigners is unrelated, and the separate-
ness of verses 11–12 is further shown by the finality of the
concluding curse in verse 12. *abominable things are done in
Israel and in Jerusalem:* 'abomination' is a term frequently
used in Deuteronomy to describe religious apostasy. *in Israel*
is probably an addition to the text which originally placed
*Judah* and *Jerusalem* in parallel. *Judah has violated the holiness
of the LORD:* this could also mean 'has violated the sanctuary
of the LORD', which could refer equally to the temple or to the
land. *by loving and marrying daughters of a foreign god:* by loving
could be applied to God's love for the 'sanctuary' if that were

[a] *So Sept.; Heb.* let him not be.

149

meant instead of *holiness*. The N.E.B. rendering is to be preferred, however. This appears to indicate a narrowly nationalistic outlook, yet the strange reference to foreign women as *daughters of a foreign god* suggests that the objection to them was religious rather than nationalistic. They are foreigners who, unlike Ruth the Moabitess, refused to become worshippers of Yahweh. Like Solomon's wives they continued to practise their own foreign cults on Israelite soil. Apostates, like the priests, are made impure even if *they bring offerings to the LORD of Hosts* and are better cut off from the community of faith, i.e. *the dwellings of Jacob. nomads or settlers:* the Hebrew words are not clear. Presumably two nouns are intended which suggest totality. It would be possible to read 'awakener or answerer', or, with slight emendation, 'witness or advocate'. This addition reflects the outlook attributed to Nehemiah and to Ezra by the Chronicler. There is nothing to tell us when it was added at this point, or by whom.

13–16. The text of these verses, especially verse 15, is obviously corrupt and very difficult to translate. However, the very bad state of the text bears its own witness to the probability that it did originally condemn divorce outright. If so, this passage is unique in the Old Testament and it would be small wonder if it suffered from scribal efforts to soften it. Divorce was never prohibited as such by Judaism, although it was regulated in Deut. 24: 1–4. A man could not simply put his wife away. He had to write a bill of divorce, no doubt giving adequate reasons.

14. *though she is your partner and your wife by solemn covenant:* a phrase which says much for the view of marriage expressed here and also for the understanding of *covenant*. A similar view of marriage as a covenant between two people witnessed by God is found in Gen. 31: 50 and Prov. 2: 16–17. Some have understood the reference to faithlessness to the covenant with *the wife of your youth* in a metaphorical sense as faithlessness to the covenant religion of Yahweh. They can appeal to

the use of the marriage metaphor to describe the covenant relationship between Yahweh and his people in Hosea and Jeremiah (e.g. Jer. 3: 20). In such cases, however, Yahweh is always portrayed as the husband. *

## GOD WILL SHOW HIMSELF IN JUDGEMENT
### AND CLEANSING

You have wearied the LORD with your talk. You ask, 17 'How have we wearied him?' By saying that all evildoers are good in the eyes of the LORD, that he is pleased with them, or by asking, 'Where is the God of justice?' Look, **3** I am sending my messenger[a] who will clear a path before me. Suddenly the Lord whom you seek will come to his temple; the messenger of the covenant in whom you delight is here, here already, says the LORD of Hosts. Who 2 can endure the day of his coming? Who can stand firm when he appears? He is like a refiner's fire, like fuller's soap; he will take his seat, refining and purifying;[b] he 3 will purify the Levites and cleanse them like gold and silver, and so they shall be fit to bring offerings to the LORD. Thus the offerings of Judah and Jerusalem shall be 4 pleasing to the LORD as they were in days of old, in years long past. I will appear before you in court, prompt to 5 testify against sorcerers, adulterers, and perjurers, against those who wrong[c] the hired labourer, the widow, and the orphan, who thrust the alien aside and have no fear of me, says the LORD of Hosts.

[a] my messenger: *Heb*. Malachi.
[b] *Prob. rdg.; Heb. adds* silver.
[c] *Prob. rdg.; Heb. adds* the wages of.

✣ 17. *You have wearied the LORD with your talk:* the passage which follows is again introduced by the prophetic dispute with the people. It draws on earlier prophetic material, presumably to say that the earlier promises are about to be fulfilled in present or imminent events. This phrase echoes Isa. 43: 24:

'...you burdened me with your sins
        and wearied me with your iniquities.'

*all evildoers are good in the eyes of the LORD...'Where is the God of justice?':* the questions are echoed again in 3: 13–15 and the reply appears to come in 3: 16–18.

3: 1. *Look, I am sending my messenger who will clear a path before me:* this seems to be an allusion to Isa. 40: 3:

'There is a voice that cries:
    Prepare a road for the LORD through the wilderness,
    clear a highway across the desert for our God.'

The messenger here may have no specific identity, the emphasis being on the appearance of God himself; or else the prophet saw himself and his ministry as that of God's messenger preparing the way for his coming. The Hebrew for 'my messenger' is *malachi*, from which the title of the book has come. Verse 1*a* and verse 5 are in the first-person speech of God. Since verse 5 follows on logically from 1*a* and verses 1*b*–4 are in the third person, the latter are probably an addition to the original oracle, elaborating it and applying it to a later situation. This would account for the present confusion between the *messenger* of 1*a*, the *Lord* in 1*b* (which is not the name of Yahweh, but the Hebrew word for 'lord') and the *messenger of the covenant* of 1*b*. Whereas verse 5 concerns itself with wrongdoers in general and continues the answer to the questions of 2: 17, verses 2–4 speak only of the Levites who, elsewhere in the book, when mentioned specifically are spoken of favourably. *Suddenly the Lord whom you seek...:* presumably a reference to Yahweh although his name is not used and the term 'lord' could be applied to a messenger. *the messenger of the covenant...is here, here already:* commentators are divided over whether this is the same messenger mentioned earlier, a separate person, an angelic messenger or equivalent to Yahweh himself. The confusion is almost certainly due to this third-person section of verses 1*b*–4 being an addition to the original text, someone later identifying himself, or another, with the messenger of verse 1*a*. The covenant could be the Sinaitic covenant, thus speaking of the election of the nation, a fact in which they certainly did take pride (*delight*). In this case the messenger would probably be thought of as a representative of the prophetic line. Or the reference could be to the covenant with Levi (2: 4–8), in which case the messenger was probably seen as a priestly or Levitical figure. Since, in the addition, the attention is mainly on the Levites, the latter is the more probable. Some have wanted to identify *the messenger of the covenant* with an historical person, such as Ezra. The evidence is lacking to make this more than conjecture. There is little to suggest that he is seen as a messianic figure, unless all the actions of verses 2–4 are assigned to him rather than to God, who is then seen as acting through an agent. This is unlikely. All that can safely be said is that in the addition of verses 1*b*–4 the messenger of 1*a* is identified with someone now on the scene who is a harbinger of the coming of God in fulfilment of the promises of the book. *in whom you delight:* this could refer equally to the messenger or the covenant, the latter being the more likely.

2. *Who can endure the day of his coming?:* the personal pronouns in verses 2–3 most naturally refer to God. *he will take his seat, refining and purifying:* God will subject the Levites as a whole to a process of refining. It is close in thought to Zech. 13: 9. Unlike that passage, however, this addition seems to believe that the Levites as a whole are capable of responding to the divine judgement and grace.

4. *Thus the offerings...shall be pleasing to the LORD as they*

*were in days of old, in years long past:* it is hard to know what period of the people's history is in mind, since the prophets before the exile so bitterly attacked their sacrifices, while Amos (5: 25) and Jeremiah (7: 22) seem to indicate their belief that there were no sacrifices earlier in the wilderness period. This addition seems to share the idealized picture of the sacrifices offered in the wilderness period given in the Priestly writing.

*5. I will appear before you in court....*: with the return to the first-person speech of God the thought turns from the Levites to the presence of God among the whole community. He will answer the objections raised in 2: 17 by judging all aspects of wrong behaviour denounced by the earlier prophets. *prompt to testify against sorcerers:* sorcerers were those who practised magic, a practice condemned in the Law (Deut. 18: 10-11) and by the prophets (Jer. 27: 9). Though their presence is amply attested in the period before the exile, it is hard to know how prominent a part they played by this time. It may be that this whole list is drawn from evils attacked by the earlier prophets and is used in a general sense. The point would be that the promises of those prophets concerning the ideal state of Israelite society would be realized in the time of salvation. ✳

### GIVE GOD HIS DUE PLACE

6  I am the LORD, unchanging; and you, too, have not
7 ceased to be sons of Jacob. From the days of your fore-
fathers you have been wayward and have not kept my laws. If you will return to me, I will return to you, says
8 the LORD of Hosts. You ask, 'How can we return?' May man defraud God, that you defraud me? You ask, 'How have we defrauded thee?' Why, in tithes and contri-
9 butions. There is a curse, a curse on you all, the whole
10 nation of you, because you defraud me. Bring the tithes

into the treasury, all of them; let there be food in my
house. Put me to the proof, says the LORD of Hosts, and
see if I do not open windows in the sky and pour a
blessing on you as long as there is need. I will forbid pests 11
to destroy the produce of your soil or make your vines
barren, says the LORD of Hosts. All nations shall count you 12
happy, for yours shall be a favoured land, says the LORD
of Hosts.

✻ 6. *I am the LORD, unchanging:* the Hebrew lays emphasis
on the personal pronoun to point the contrast with the
people. God does not change in his love and goodness. *and
you, too, have not ceased to be sons of Jacob:* the people also have
not changed, but in their case it has been only to remain
constant in evil. There is probably a play on words. *Jacob* is
related to a word which means 'to cheat'. The verb 'to rob',
rendered 'defraud' in verses 8–9, is similar in appearance to
the word 'to cheat', and this is the reading of the Septuagint
there. The people have always been 'cheaters'.

8. *in tithes and contributions: a tithe* is a tenth, and the offering
of a tenth by a dependant to his superior is a very ancient
custom (e.g. Gen. 14: 20). The law regulating the religious
offering of tithes appears in Deut. 14: 22–9 and 26: 12–15.
What Malachi urges, however, appears to be closer to the
provisions of the Priestly Code than to Deuteronomy (see
Lev. 27: 30–3; Num. 18: 21–31). The word for *contributions*
is used of gifts offered for the upkeep of the temple and its
personnel.

10. *let there be food in my house:* that is, for the needs of the
priests and Levites. As Haggai made the building of the
temple a test of their concern for God, so Malachi makes their
willingness to pay for its upkeep a test of their integrity
towards God. It is equivalent to a conversion from the ways of
their forefathers and is seen as a 'return' to God (verse 7). He
does not urge obedience in ritual matters as an end in itself.

*see if I do not open windows in the sky and pour a blessing on you as long as there is need:* as with Haggai, obedience is seen as the precondition for experiencing God's blessing, which is expressed in terms of the fertility of the soil. The reference to *windows in the sky* through which God allows the waters to pour which were once pressed back behind the firmament, or 'vault' (Gen. 1: 6–8) can be used both as a picture of judgement (Gen. 8: 2) and of blessing, as here.

12. *All nations shall count you happy:* there is no thought here of the nations sharing in their blessing, as in Zech. 14: 16–19.

This dispute is addressed to the community at large and is the first to offer a conditional promise of blessing. It is almost as though the prophet sees the judging of the priesthood (1: 6 – 2: 9) as a pre-condition for a spiritual renewal of the people. ✳

# Murmurers warned, the righteous triumphant

13 YOU HAVE USED HARD WORDS about me, says the Lord, and then you ask, 'How have we spoken
14 against thee?' You have said, 'It is useless to serve God; what do we gain from the Lord of Hosts by observing
15 his rules and behaving with deference? We ourselves count the arrogant happy; it is evildoers who are successful; they have put God to the proof and come to no harm.'

16 Then those who feared the Lord talked together, and the Lord paid heed and listened. A record was written before him of those who feared him and kept his name in
17 mind. They shall be mine, says the Lord of Hosts, my

own possession against the day that I appoint, and I will
spare them as a man spares the son who serves him. You 18
will again tell good men from bad, the servant of God
from the man who does not serve him.

The day comes, glowing like a furnace; all the arrogant **4** 1ᵃ
and the evildoers shall be chaff, and that day when it
comes shall set them ablaze, says the LORD of Hosts, it
shall leave them neither root nor branch. But for you 2
who fear my name, the sun of righteousness shall rise with
healing in his wings, and you shall break loose like calves
released from the stall. On the day that I act, you shall 3
trample down the wicked, for they will be ashes under
the soles of your feet, says the LORD of Hosts.

✻ 14. *You have said, 'It is useless to serve God...':* an echo of
the doubts expressed in 2: 17. This, and the differentiation
in this section between those who 'feared the LORD' and the
'arrogant' and 'evildoers', suggests that it is the evildoers
who question God's ways.

16. *Then those who feared the LORD talked together:* the
Septuagint links the God-fearers with the murmurers of
verses 13–15 by reading, 'thus those who feared the LORD
talked together'. What is significant is the concept opening
up of a division within Judaism between evildoers on the one
side, and a community of the faithful on the other. Such a
view develops hand-in-hand with a strongly eschatological
outlook which, as here, sees the final day of Yahweh as the
occasion for revealing what is 'good' and what 'bad'. Perhaps
the reference to *those who feared the LORD* talking together
may even refer to the ministry of the prophet and those who
gathered round him and responded to his teaching. The
phrase is reminiscent of the report of the effects of Haggai's
words in the editorial framework of the book (Hag. 1: 12–15).

[a] *3: 19 in Heb.*

*A record was written before him....:* the Hebrew is 'a book of remembrance', suggesting the idea that God keeps those who fear him 'in mind'. Their names are always before him. Such an idea is found elsewhere in the Old Testament (e.g. Exod. 32: 32–3; Ps. 69: 28). The idea may come from the use of such records by kings of the ancient world (Esther 6: 1–2).

17. *my own possession against the day I appoint:* the word rendered *possession* implies a very valued property. It is nearly always applied to Israel as the object of God's electing grace, often being parallel to the word 'choose'. Here it is applied, not to Israel as a whole, but to the faithful. Unlike Zech. 14 Malachi portrays them as being spared the judgement to come against the wicked on the day of Yahweh.

4: 1. *The day comes, glowing like a furnace:* fire is often a picture of the presence and judgement of God (e.g. Amos 7: 4). Here it is not a 'refining fire' as in 3: 2 (another indication that 3: 2 is an addition to the book), but a fire which, by destroying the wicked utterly, will bring to light the differences of faith and piety which already exist among the people of the nation.

2. *the sun of righteousness shall rise with healing in his wings:* the only use of this picture in the Old Testament, although God is pictured as a sun, shining in blessing on his people (Ps. 84: 11, rendered differently in the N.E.B.). Perhaps there is an echo of the Aaronic blessing in Num. 6: 24–6. Again, the references in the Psalms to God's help coming 'in the morning' (e.g. Ps. 30: 5) may have suggested this idea of his coming to help being like the sun rising after the night of distress. The wings refer to the portrayal of the winged solar disc in Egyptian and Mesopotamian art. The sun god thus pictured was known as the 'judge' among the gods of the pantheon, and so it is fitting that Yahweh is pictured as rising like the sun to establish righteousness. *you shall break loose like calves released from the stall:* a vivid picture of the joy of the faithful at the time of salvation.

3. *you shall trample down the wicked...:* to the modern reader this note on which the original book ended may seem rather vindictive. Nevertheless, it promises that all evil shall be rooted out of the community. This assurance brings to a climax the mingled threats and promises of the book.  *

CONCLUDING EXHORTATION AND PROMISES

Remember the law of Moses my servant, the rules and 4 precepts which I bade him deliver to all Israel at Horeb.

Look, I will send you the prophet Elijah before the 5 great and terrible day of the LORD comes. He will 6 reconcile fathers to sons and sons to fathers, lest I come and put the land under a ban to destroy it.

* 4. *Remember the law of Moses my servant:* this verse, which relates neither to what has preceded it nor to what follows, is a later exhortation added to the book, just as an unknown writer added an exhortation to the book of Hosea (Hos. 14: 9). It is in the style of Deuteronomy. Deuteronomy uses *Remember* in this sense of not only recalling the law but living in obedience to it; it refers to Moses as the *servant* of God (e.g. Deut. 34: 5); it often refers to the law as *the rules and precepts*, or 'statutes and laws' as in the N.E.B. translation of Deuteronomy (e.g. Deut. 4: 1, 8); the phrase *all Israel* is Deuteronomic (Deut. 5: 1), and Deuteronomy and the Elohist call the mountain of the law *Horeb*, where the Yahwist and the Priestly writers call it Sinai. The reference is probably to the Torah as a whole and so represents a late stage when it had achieved its final form and gained authority. The only other use of the phrase the *law of Moses* is found in the book of Daniel (Dan. 9: 11, 13), also a later work. The addition attempts to unite law and prophets as equally authoritative coming as it does, not only at the end of the book of Malachi, but at the end of 'The Book of the Twelve', as the collection

of the so-called 'minor prophets' from Hosea to Malachi
came to be known.

*5–6. Look, I will send you the prophet Elijah . . . :* this appears
to refer back to Mal. 3: 1, attempting to identify the messenger. Yet his role is different from that of the messenger of
Malachi. That messenger needed only to 'clear a path' for
God, who would then come to differentiate between the
faithful and the wicked and to pass sentence on the latter (3: 5).
Here the prophet Elijah has an active ministry to perform in
preparing the community for God's own coming later by a
work of reconciliation among them. Elijah may be singled out
because of the tradition that he had not died but had been
caught up into heaven (2 Kings 2: 1–12). Again, he was the
first major prophet of the Old Testament and he may symbolize the promise of a renewal of prophecy to prepare the
people for the last time, at a period when the living voice of
prophecy had faded. He was also remembered in the tradition
for saving the faith of Yahwism at a time of religious apostasy,
crisis and even persecution. This would make his a very
fitting ministry if this addition dated from the time of persecution under Antiochus IV (Epiphanes). This belief in a
return of Elijah before the coming day of the LORD was taken
up in later Jewish writings (e.g. Ecclus. 48: 10) and finds
expression in the New Testament (e.g. Mark 6: 15; 15: 35).
*before the great and terrible day of the LORD comes:* this continues the prophetic theme of the Day of Yahweh as a 'day of
darkness' (e.g. Amos 5: 18–20). It is close to the description
of the day in Joel 2: 11, 31 and may suggest that this addition,
like chs. 2 and 3 of the book of Joel reflects a growingly
apocalyptic-type eschatology. *He will reconcile fathers to sons
and sons to fathers:* unlike the rest of the book of Malachi this
does not recognize the division which the coming of God will
reveal as between good and bad, but sees the whole community as being in danger of judgement because of its inner
tensions and divisions. The fact that *fathers and sons* are mentioned could reflect the conditions of the Greek period when

the younger generation grasped eagerly at Greek customs and thought, to the horror of their more orthodox parents. Or it may reflect the writer's view of a community just generally at odds within itself, a view confirmed by the Septuagint which adds another phrase, 'he shall turn the heart of a father to a son, and the heart of a man to his neighbour'. It may therefore express the belief that the condition of society in his own time fulfils words like Isa. 3: 5:

> 'the people shall deal harshly
> each man with his fellow and with his neighbour;
> children shall break out against their elders,
> and nobodies against men of substance.'

The role of Elijah is to exercise a ministry which will recall the community to right ways and so prepare it as a whole for God's coming. *lest I come and put the land under a ban to destroy it:* otherwise the whole community is in danger of destruction, for the ban, which meant basically offering something wholly to God, involved total destruction of a city and its inhabitants (e.g. Josh. 6: 17). It means that the threat against Edom in 1: 3–4 is in danger of falling on the people of Judah as well unless they respond to the call which God will give them through the prophet to come. The writer of this addition, at least, saw 1: 1–5 as containing a conditional warning for the 'chosen' people themselves.

It seems a harsh note on which to end, not only the book of Malachi, but also 'The Book of the Twelve'. Indeed, in our English Bible these are the final words of the Old Testament, although in the Jewish Bible the Prophets were followed by the Writings. It may be for this reason that the Septuagint altered the order by putting verse 4 as the final words of the book, following verses 5–6, while in Jewish liturgy it became the custom in public reading to repeat verse 5 after verse 6.

Nevertheless, it is in some ways a fitting, if stern, conclusion to the collection of the prophetic books. It reminded the hearers and readers that the ministry of the prophets was a preparation for God's coming to his people so that they might enter into the joy of salvation rather than experience his judgement. In this way Elijah here may be said to symbolize the ministry of the prophets as a whole. The prophets' words were not to provide food for idle curiosity. They confronted their contemporary hearers and later readers with the challenge of the need for a response. ✳

# A NOTE ON FURTHER READING

There are few recent commentaries on the books of Haggai, Zechariah and Malachi in English. One brief one, which is written from a conservative point of view but takes note of much recent work in French and German, is that in the Tyndale Old Testament Commentaries by Joyce G. Baldwin (Inter-Varsity Press, 1972). Useful background material can be found in two volumes of the New Clarendon Bible (Oxford University Press): P. R. Ackroyd, *Israel under Babylon and Persia* (1970) and D. S. Russell, *The Jews from Alexander to Herod* (1967). A more advanced work dealing with much of the material covered in this commentary, although from a very distinctive standpoint, is that by P. D. Hanson, *The Dawn of Apocalyptic: the Historical and Sociological Roots of Jewish Apocalyptic Eschatology* (Fortress, 1975). Much of the Qumran literature can be found in G. Vermes, *The Dead Sea Scrolls in English* (2nd ed., Penguin Books, 1975).

# INDEX

Abraham 149

Absalom 119, 125

Alexander the Great 80, 84

Amos 29, 50, 84–5, 122, 124, 160

angels: the 'interpreting' angel 35–6, 45; angel of the LORD 35–6, 50, 51, 117

Antiochus IV (Epiphanes) 160

apocalyptic 76–7, 112, 134

Arabah 128

Aram (Syria) 84

Asal 126

Ashdod 85–6

Ashkelon 86

Assyria 101

Babylon 1, 3, 4, 5, 12, 14, 27, 30, 37, 40, 43, 58, 59, 60; neo-Babylonian Empire 1, 3

Baruch 7

Bathsheba 119

Beersheba 129

Berechiah 27

Bethel-Sharezer 65–6

Boaz (pillar in Solomon's temple) 59–60

branch (as messianic term) 51–2, 63

Cambyses 5–6

Chronicler 4, 5, 9, 10, 14, 22, 25, 32, 39, 67, 70, 74–5, 137, 138, 150

Chronicles 4, 9

covenant 17, 43, 57, 91–2, 133, 147, 149, 150–1, 152–3

Cyrus 3, 4, 5; the 'Cyrus Cylinder' 4

Damascus 84

*Damascus Rule, The* 85

Darius I (Hystaspes) 6, 14, 19, 25, 32, 35, 37, 65

David 14, 25, 86, 119, 125; hopes concerning a coming descendant of David 25, 52, 117

Day of the LORD 160

Dead Sea 128

Deuteronomy 43, 57, 116, 130, 138, 140, 146, 149, 150, 155, 159

'deutero-Zechariah' 10–11, 76–82, 133–4, 138–9; resemblances to Zechariah 1–8, 10–11, 78–9

Dispersion (Diaspora) 47, 60, 62, 73, 75, 101, 124

diviners 97

divorce 135, 150

Ecclesiasticus 137

Edom 136, 138, 140–2, 161

Egypt 2, 4, 100, 101, 102, 110; exodus from 3, 20, 42

Ekron 86

Eliakim 100

Elijah 160–1, 162

Elohist 159

ephah (N.E.B. 'barrel') 57–8

Ephraim 89, 93

Esau 141; *see also* Edom

eschatology 76–7, 138, 157

Euphrates 102

Exodus, book of 20

exodus from Egypt 3, 20, 42

Ezekiel 3, 28, 29–30, 38, 39, 57, 58, 73, 74, 80, 85, 97, 99, 106–10, 111, 115–18, 120, 124–5, 128, 147–8

Ezra 138, 150, 153

Ezra; book of 5, 14

Gaza 86

Geba 129

Gedaliah 67, 72

Gilead 102

God: activity in history 7; glory of 16, 21, 38, 42, 43, 124–5; grace of 2, 28; kingship of 25, 45, 60, 77, 83–5, 96, 122–3, 127–9 132, 145; nature of according to Second Isaiah 3; presence of, in Jerusalem

# INDEX

Megiddo 119

messenger formula 15

messianic hopes: attached to the 'branch' 51–2, 63; to the coming king 87–90; to Zerubbabel, 25, 28; 'democratised' 117

Micah 136

Molech 125

Moses 9, 18, 20, 159

Mount of Olives 124–5

Nathan 120

Nehemiah 106, 137–8, 144, 150

Nehemiah, book of 4, 14

New Year festival 89, 96, 115, 132

Noah 128

Obadiah 140–1

Onias III 119

Palestine 1, 3

peace (*shalom*) 21, 90

Pentateuch 3, 9, 18

Persian Empire 3, 5, 6, 25

Peshitta (Syriac version of Old Testament) 56

Philistines 83, 85, 86, 87, 116, 132

pit 92

Priestly writing 9, 10, 18, 138, 143, 148, 155, 159

priests, priesthood 10, 22, 25, 28, 50–1, 143, 155; Aaronites 147, 148; Zadokites 148; attacked by Malachi 135, 146–8; cultic role of priests in the temple after the exile 66; dominance after the exile 52, 63, 75; high priest, mediating role of 54, turban 51, 132–3; priests as 'false shepherds' 97, 109

prophecy 28

prophetic disputation 15, 136, 140, 143, 152, 156

prophets 3, 6–8, 15, 28, 29–31, 32–3, 66, 67, 76–9, 103, 105, 120, 121–2, 135, 154; acts of prophetic symbolism 104–10, 111; cultic role in temple after the exile 66; the end of prophets in the future age 121–

2; false prophets attacked 97–8; prophetic 'schools' or 'disciples' 7–8; as 'watchmen' 29–31

Proverbs, book of 3

Psalms 12, 25, 30–1, 89–90, 92, 103, 115, 120, 128–9, 132, 144–5, 158

Qumran Community 134

rain (as sign of eschatological blessing) 96, 132

Regem-Melech 65–6

'remnant' 5, 8, 17, 26, 69, 71, 74, 111, 112, 124

Rimmon 129

Ruth 150

sacrifice 135, 143, 144–5, 153–4

Samaria 14; Samaritans 65

Samson 116

Satan (the Adversary) 50

Second Isaiah 3, 4, 36, 37, 42, 74, 88–90, 92–3, 94–5, 101, 108, 115, 125, 136, 152

Seleucids 84

Septuagint (Greek version of Old Testament) 20, 22, 55, 58, 89, 125, 141, 157, 161

Seraiah 14

Servant 87–90, 93

Shalmaneser 84

Sharezer, *see* Bethel-shareser

Shealtiel 14

Sheol 92

Sheshbazzar 5, 144

Shimei 120

Shinar 58

Sidon 85

Sinai, Mount of 20, 159

Sinaitic covenant 91, 153–5

Solomon 5, 52, 125, 150

sorcerers 154

spirit of God, *see* God, spirit of

Tabernacles, Feast of, *see* New Year festival

targum 87

taunt-song 103

167

# INDEX

temple 2, 5, 6, 9, 10, 12, 14, 16, 19, 20, 21, 22, 23, 25, 26, 27, 28, 29, 32, 37, 41, 42, 43, 44, 45, 47, 48, 51, 52, 54, 55, 56, 57, 58, 59, 60, 62, 63, 64, 66, 69, 70, 71, 72, 74, 75, 87, 108–9, 112, 128, 135, 136, 137, 139, 141
teraphim 96–7
theocracy 26
theophany, *see* God, presence of (theophany)
Tiglath-Pileser III 84
tithes 136, 138, 154–6
Torah 159
Tyre 80, 85

universalism: and Haggai 20–1; and Zechariah, 1–8, 28, 72–4, 75–9, 108; and Zechariah, 9–14, 77, 79, 86, 88–90; and Malachi 141–2, 144–5
Uzziah 126

Vulgate (Latin version of Old Testament) 20

Wisdom literature 3
wise men 97

Yahweh 2, 15, 48; Yahwism 2, 160; Yahwist 159

Zechariah 1, 4, 5, 6, 10–11, 27–8, 30–1, 62, 73–4
Zechariah, book of 4, 10, 25; its editorial framework 10, 29, 32–4, 35, 47–8, 52, 54–6, 63–4, 67, 70–3, 74–5; night visions 29–31
Zechariah 9–14, *see* 'deutero-Zechariah'
Zechariah ben Jeberechiah 27
Zerubbabel 5, 6, 10, 14, 25, 28, 45–6, 48, 52, 54–5, 62–3, 74–5, 144

## DATE DUE